Praise for

Sometimes He Whispers
Sometimes He Roars

"God wants to hear our hearts, share our pain, and reveal Himself through prayer, which is the cornerstone of our relationship with Him. But prayer is also the catalyst that God uses to move mountains, change the hearts of kings, and impact nations. Marilynn's book, *Sometimes He Whispers Sometimes He Roars,* is a clarion call to pray effectively and powerfully as we learn to hear the voice and understand the heart of a Father who loves us beyond our imagining."

—Terry Meeuwsen, cohost of *The 700 Club*

"I was very encouraged to read Marilynn's personal stories of answered prayer. She challenged me to do my own 21-Day Experiment. I have a crazy, busy schedule and the *Sometimes He Whispers Sometimes He Roars* helped bring discipline and structure to my prayer life. Even coaches need a coach and Marilynn provided some great coaching for me. Hers is an example of a life well lived."

—David Marsh, two-time US Olympic swimming coach;
former NCAA championship coach at Auburn University;
president and CEO of Mecklenburg Aquatic Club

"Marilynn Chadwick has provided timeless insights into the discipline of prayer in a way that is simple, sincere, and practical. Marilynn inspires both novices and experienced Christians to partner with God on a daily basis through moments of listening to and obeying God's whispering or roaring voices. I recommend this revolutionary book, *Sometimes He Whispers Sometimes He Roars,* to

Christians who long to hear the voice of God for their lives, their families, their communities, and the nations."

—Celestin Musekura, Ph.D., founder and president of the African Leadership and Reconciliation Ministry; author of *Forgiving as We've Been Forgiven*

"After reading Marilynn's *Sometimes He Whispers Sometimes He Roars,* I now find myself looking forward to my daily prayer times. I love the book's practical nature, which helped me create a prayer pattern that was well suited to my personality. The book challenged me to become more intentional not only about my own prayer life but also about praying together with my husband. I have become more aware of the incredible privilege we have to pray and the confidence we can have to know the Lord answers prayer and rewards those who earnestly seek Him."

—Laura Kasay, wife of NFL player John Kasay

"Marilynn's book, *Sometimes He Whispers Sometimes He Roars,* will inspire you and give you the direction you need to build a solid foundation for overcoming the obstacles of life. She shares her personal journey in her search for the heart of God. Her findings are the answers we all need. As you travel through the pages of this book, you will be encouraged and you will grow in faith, knowing you too can be an over-comer."

—Linda Hendrick, wife of NASCAR owner Rick Hendrick

Sometimes He
WHISPERS
Sometimes He
ROARS

Sometimes He
WHISPERS
Sometimes He
ROARS

❖

Learning to Hear the Voice of God

MARILYNN CHADWICK

HOWARD BOOKS
A DIVISION OF SIMON & SCHUSTER, INC.
New York • Nashville • London • Toronto • Sydney • New Delhi

Howard Books
A Division of Simon & Schuster, Inc.
1230 Avenue of the Americas
New York, NY 10020

First Howard Books trade paperback edition January 2012

HOWARD and colophon are trademarks of Simon & Schuster, Inc.

For information about special discounts for bulk purchases, please contact Simon & Schuster Special Sales at 1-866-506-1949 or business@simonandschuster.com.

The Simon & Schuster Speakers Bureau can bring authors to your live event. For more information or to book an event contact the Simon & Schuster Speakers Bureau at 1-866-248-3049 or visit our website at www.simonspeakers.com.

Designed by Renato Stanisic

Manufactured in the United States of America

10 9 8 7 6 5 4 3 2 1

Library of Congress Cataloging-in-Publication Data

Chadwick, Marilynn.
Sometimes He whispers sometimes He roars : learning to hear the voice of God / Marilynn Chadwick.
  p. cm.
  Includes bibliographical references (p.).
  1. Prayer—Christianity. I. Title.
  BV215.C46 2012
  248.3'2—dc23   2011038139

ISBN 978-1-4516-5736-4

TO DAVID,
MY KIND-HEARTED, BASKETBALL-PLAYER-TURNED-
PREACHER HUSBAND
—AND THE LOVE OF MY LIFE

Contents

Contents

Sometimes He

WHISPERS

Sometimes He

ROARS

Introduction

Survivor.

We hear that word a lot these days. Survivors have stories—and usually a few secrets to share with us. Especially about how they made it out of whatever it was they faced—alive. Some of you have had your own "uh-oh, this may be my last breath of life" moments. I want to tell you about mine.

My brush with death came more than a decade ago on a quiet Saturday morning in February. Our youngest, Michael, was four at the time. We were headed to the beach for a quick overnighter. My husband, David, and our other two children, Bethany and David Banner, had various work and sports commitments, so Michael and I launched out on our own little beach adventure—just the two of us. It was an unseasonably warm weekend, well worth the four-hour drive to enjoy the North Carolina coast. I was ready for a day of sea and sunshine. Besides, the beach is my favorite place and Michael is a beach lover, too.

We got an early start and stopped about an hour outside of Charlotte, at the Burger King in Wadesboro on Highway 74, headed for the coast. After going in to buy a quick kids' breakfast and refilling my coffee cup, we walked back to the car, eager to get on the road. Once in the parking lot, I turned around and motioned to Michael to hurry up. I wondered why this normally cooperative child just stood there on the curb holding his little bag of breakfast with an odd look on his face. A split second later, I knew why. My world suddenly exploded in pain as I was hit by a van backing up—rather quickly I might add.

The experience seemed to happen in slow motion, but I was more able to think than I would have imagined. My first thought was, *You are being hit hard by a van.* (Instinctively I knew it was a van because it hit me in the head as well as my back.) *Secondly, the driver is still backing up and doesn't know you are here, so scream, and LOUDLY.* Now, this is significant because by nature, I am not a screamer. But I screamed—bloody murder. The van backed over me. Thankfully I was in between and not under the wheels. After what seemed like an eternity, the van finally came to a halt. Everything rushed, but in slow motion.

The woman who hit me (she looked like a soccer mom also on her way to the beach) jumped out of the van—horrified. A crowd quickly assembled. Bleeding, I hopped up off the pavement, with injured knees and elbows, frantically looking around for my son.

I found Michael sitting by himself on the curb, so I went over and sat down beside my trembling child. I was more worried about this little four-year-old who just watched his mother get plowed over by a minivan than I was about myself. I resisted the offer of the EMTs to take me to the hospital in the pickup truck that was the rescue vehicle on duty in Wadesboro that morning—though I did let them bandage my wounds.

I thanked the kind bystanders and the Burger King workers who brought Michael a fresh Happy Meal. Then, I got back in my car, with my bruised and broken body, and slowly drove the remaining three hours to the beach. I was determined to make sure my little son had his day at the beach to erase the memory of what he said was "the worst day of my life."

We ended up buying another Happy Meal that night, so he could wait forty-five minutes with me in the emergency room after my elbow swelled to three times its size. My arm turned black and blue—an ugly hematoma—but no broken bones.

Before Michael dropped off to sleep the next evening, after a peaceful day enjoying the beach, he said, "Mom, this was the best day of my life!" I guess that's how God made four-year-olds.

And God made mothers to cope with crises. Most people, when faced with a life-and-death moment, discover that there is an incredible will to live—to survive. Journalist Laurence Gonzales has done decades of research into discovering why some people survive and others perish. Gonzales found that survivors tend to exhibit several behaviors. Simply stated, survivors "breathe," they "organize," and they "act."[1]

They take a moment to breathe and reflect, rather than plunging immediately into panic or impulse (*Gee, I've just been hit by a minivan*). They formulate a plan (*Better scream loudly*), then they take action (*Scream!*). Those who survive also tend to discover that caring for someone else more than themselves (*I've got to comfort my child*) is an important factor in survival and its aftermath.

Less than a year after my accident, I would find myself walking through another variation of the "breathe—organize—act" response, but not for myself. I was simply one of the millions around the world who sat stunned as we watched the World Trade Center attack on 9/11. And while my personal safety did not hang in the balance, I knew that life as we knew it would never be the same.

Gonzales's survival behaviors are remarkably like some patterns that emerged in my own response to the tragedy. Just like the majority of Americans, my first response was to pray. Instinctively, I took time to "breathe," and sensed God calling me to be alert—to watch, listen, and pray for our nation, and beyond. I "organized" a strategy to pray that included a detailed list along with methods of praying the promises of God's Word. I "took action" by tapping into teamwork and exploring ways I could be the answer to other people's prayers. I didn't realize it then, but September 11 ignited a personal journey that would ultimately change the trajectory of my life. But the real story is about God. He was calling me to become an active prayer warrior for a hurting and broken world that He deeply loves.

In the course of this journey—a journey that I know beyond a doubt was God ordained—I saw amazing answers to personal prayers for my own family. But I also found myself moving outside my world of comfort. I discovered a world beyond my own that led me to places and people I never knew even existed, beginning with my own community. I didn't know where I was going at the time—I only tried to be faithful to listen to God on a daily basis.

But patterns began to form and I quickly realized that this journey was taking me somewhere. There was a method, and there was purpose. So I began marking the path, and soon enough, I began teaching others how to follow the steps themselves.

Technically speaking, there are six steps laid out in this book to developing a deeper and more effective prayer life. But the important thing to note is that all of the parts are interrelated. They are not mutually exclusive—rather, they depend on one another. So you will notice, throughout the book, that although each chapter will have a main theme, I will often mention some or all of the other parts within that chapter, because all six steps coexist in harmony. In time, I think you'll find that the steps will help you develop your own rhythm of prayer.

With God's help and grace, I have been developing these steps for nearly ten years, since just after 9/11. They began as a journey, and they happened neither perfectly chronologically nor without trial and error. But I know this: they have revolutionized my prayer life, as well as my everyday life, into something more powerful and wondrous than I could have imagined. Nothing's perfect, but with prayer, it is *good*.

Here are the steps I followed, in a nutshell. We'll go over them in much greater detail in the following chapters.

1. *Be Alert.* The first thing I learned was that I needed to be alert not only to God's voice but to the needs all around me. Being alert meant I was intentional about listening for God's voice, watching for signs of His work. This is no small order in an era that is too busy, too noisy, and often numbed out by ever-pressing demands.

2. *Be Specific.* The calling to pray for the world is a tall order, and awareness of that call taught me what it means to be specific when I ask God to act on my behalf or on behalf of others. How specific was I to be? Specific enough so I would recognize the answers as they came.

3. *Pray with Authority.* Learning how to pray God's Word into situations gave solid footing to my prayers. And that gave me biblical authority—which only added power to my prayers. I took lessons from God's Instruction Book and found mentors in some of the world changers like Elijah, Peter, and Paul. And the best training tips came straight from Jesus Himself.

4. *Agree with Others in Prayer.* Don't go this alone, God implored me. So I learned the power of agreement with others in prayer.
5. *Arm Yourself with Spiritual Strength.* Life is full of spiritual as well as earthly battles. It is important, I learned, to arm myself with spiritual strength for the spiritual war that incessantly wages behind the scenes.
6. *Answer God's Call.* Pretty soon into this journey I realized that the point of all this was not simply to find one more prayer technique or add one more Bible study method to my already tall stack. If that's all that came of this journey, then "so what"? I kept telling myself that my life was either a "so what" or a "so that." I wanted to grow in my understanding of prayer and sharpen my listening. The point of all this was so that I could be useful to God. I wanted to answer God's call to go into the world with the good news of Jesus Christ and to share His love with the least and the lost.

One of the places my personal pray journey has taken me, several times over, is Africa. I'll explain more throughout the book, but for now, I'll share this. The Africans have a word, *sankofa,* which means "to walk forward while looking back." This describes my journey quite well. As I look back over the last ten years, the steps have emerged somewhat clearly in retrospect, though at the time, I was only feeling my way along.

In common vernacular, *sankofa* also can mean this: "It is not taboo to go back and fetch what one forgot." As part of the six steps in prayer, I've included some lessons I've learned in my larger journey of thirty-plus years of walking with Christ. I went back in my memory bank and "fetched" some of what I had forgotten. So you'll read about my life as a coed at a large southern university in the seventies, when I was more absorbed with fun, football games, and finding myself than I was with finding God. I'll tell of what I learned about persevering in prayer during years of struggling with infertility—and celebrations of God's victories when David and my three children were born. There was much I went back to "fetch." Not a drop was wasted.

Just what can prayer do? I agree with nineteenth-century author E. M. Bounds, who said, "Prayer can do anything God can do." I learned that if you truly commit your heart to God and are willing to be used by Him in prayer, miraculous things can happen.

The following book is a collection of footprints I've left as I've walked this journey with God. But I must be clear: there is lots of room for your own creative mind to tweak, reconfigure, or discard parts of my particular pattern. If I can catch a glimpse of God at work both in my own backyard and around the world, I think this adventure is available to anyone, in any way God desires.

God, I had prayed on the morning of 9/11, *what would happen if I committed to pray for your world?* This story is the journey that followed.

PART ONE

Be Alert

Chapter 1

Listen

The end of all things is near. You must be self-controlled and alert, to be able to pray.

—1 Peter 4:7, GNT

Like the rest of the world, I was shocked by the sudden violence and hatred aimed at America's people on 9/11. Two hijacked passenger jets-turned-missiles found their civilian target by hitting the twin towers of the World Trade Center, and soon afterward desperate office workers hurled themselves out of skyscraper windows hundreds of feet above the street as their buildings were engulfed in flames. Then those mammoth obelisks began to crumble in a heap of ash and smoke.

A surprise attack killing thousands of innocent citizens on American soil? I sat transfixed, watching over and over as news stations replayed the horrific scenario. Unthinkable.

Feeling overcome by fear and worry, I finally turned off the television and retreated to the quiet of my car. Bible in hand, I asked God to take away my fear and give me faith—and wisdom. No one really knew what we faced at that point. Nor did we know the source of the attacks. I was fearful for my family and my country as I thought about possible dangers in the days ahead. Nothing like this had ever happened on America's soil. How could we have been so sound asleep? I grieved for the many who had lost loved ones in the attack, and I shuddered to think what this meant for years to come. Our sense of peace and security had gone up in smoke. In a matter of minutes, we had suddenly become a nation at war.

Helpless, I simply asked God to show me how to respond. I wasn't a soldier, just an ordinary wife and mother. How could I possibly protect those I loved? What could I do to help defend our nation? I began to feel the weight of concern for God's people all over the earth. Gradually, the following thought came as a whisper: *God, what would happen if I committed to praying for Your world?* I wanted to believe that miracles could happen. But did I? What could one person do?

SEARCHING THE BIBLE FOR INSTRUCTIONS

Over the years, I had seen amazing answers to prayer. I had also learned from experience that God could be trusted to speak to me through the pages of Scripture. It's no wonder that the Bible is referred to as being "living and active" (Hebrews 4:12). God's Word never failed to strengthen my faith and remove fear. I sure needed help now.

I began reading from 1 Peter, which was a letter addressed to early Christians who were facing great danger and persecution. Obviously, we were also facing great danger, so I wanted to see how Peter responded. In the letter, he shares survival secrets for what to do when times look darkest. "The end of all things is near," he writes. Therefore, "be self-controlled and alert" so that you can pray (1 Peter 4:7 GNT).

It had sure felt like the end of my world when I was watching the twin towers crumble in smoke. How odd, I noted, that Peter's advice was not to run and hide, build a bomb shelter, panic, or fight, but to pray.

And it was equally odd that the encouragement was not to have passion or power as a starting point, but rather self-control and alertness. As I pondered the passage from 1 Peter, I reasoned that in order for prayer to be as powerful as the Bible seems to promise, it needed to include a measure of precision, skill, and discipline. I envisioned a brain surgeon enduring years of education, training, and practice to develop the precision to operate in the delicate minefields of the mind, knowing just where to cut. I was eager to learn more about just how and where to focus my prayers, and for whom.

In the quiet of my car, I purposed then and there that I would begin to pray with more practice and precision—and although I wasn't a soldier, I'd sign up for a "tour of duty," to be available to God in prayer, not just for my own needs and worries, but for the worries of the world. And since I hadn't a clue as to what this should look like, I asked God to guide me. But how could I hear the voice of God amid all the chaos and turmoil in my head after the terrorist attacks? I continued to search the pages of the Bible. There I discovered another prayer mentor in the prophet Elijah.

THE SECOND VOICE

Elijah is described in the book of James as being human "just like us" (James 5:17). Yet Elijah "prayed earnestly" that it wouldn't rain for three and a half years, and it didn't. Then he reversed his prayer, praying for rain—and "the heavens gave rain." His prayers had impact on an entire nation. The prayers of even one righteous person, James tells us, are "powerful and effective."

But I was curious. The Bible teaches us that no one is "perfectly righteous." I paused for a moment, reminding myself of what I knew to be my only solid footing for prayer—the righteousness that comes by faith in Jesus Christ (Romans 3:22, 23). This understanding was crucial to my confidence in prayer.

Elijah was known as a man who listened to God, and over the course of my prayer journey, I returned to his story often for instruction. Repeatedly in the Bible, we read that "the word of the Lord came to Elijah." He saw miracle after miracle as he stepped out in obedience to God's voice. I was sure Elijah would have plenty to teach me about how to pray during a time of crisis. The prophet had also faced his own personal battle with terror. After an enormous fight of faith in which he defeated a demonized mob of over four hundred prophets of Baal, Elijah was the target of a death threat by the wicked Queen Jezebel.

Elijah's deliverance came as he ultimately learned to hear God, not in the earthquake, wind, or fire, but in a gentle whisper. I sensed I should listen for God, too, not in the fiery drama that was unfolding after the terrorist attacks, but rather in "the still, small voice" of my heart. Somehow, I just knew that if God were to give me instructions about how to pray, it would not be in the *first* voice—the tumultuous roar I heard in my head, with its temptation to panic—but rather in the *second* voice, a voice of calm and reason.

Practically speaking, I began to make some life changes to help me become more alert. If God was speaking, I wanted to be ready to listen. And like Elijah, I needed to find a way to get quiet enough to hear God's whispers. Unfortunately, I had a weakness in keeping a schedule, and especially in getting up in the morning.

Help to get me out of bed came in the form of a running buddy. My next-door neighbor, Susan, a nurse practitioner and busy mother of three, had discovered that 5:30 a.m. was a great time to jump-start her day. She invited me to run with her. *Impossible!* was my first thought. I could hardly pull myself out of bed at 7 a.m. to get the children to school. No way could I get up at 5:15. But I had promised God. Our world was in turmoil. I wanted to pray more than I wanted to sleep. And so I agreed.

That first morning, the brutal alarm clock went off, and I awakened in a fog at 5:15. *If I can just get my shoes on*, I groaned out of my sleep coma. For a couple of weeks, morning felt like a death sentence. *How could I do this to myself?* But the two-mile run began to refresh me. The dark moods that sometimes hovered at the edge of my mornings became less frequent. And gradually, morning runs became easier, even joyful. Kind of like bikers who draft behind a fast-moving truck, I "drafted" behind my friend Susan in those early days of forming the habit of a morning run and prayer. I couldn't have done it without the help of my faithful teammate.

Best of all, I returned home by six, with plenty of time to have unhurried quiet to read my Bible and pray before everyone awakened. "I may be barely alive at five," I would tell myself, "but I will be great by eight!" Or, "Don't evaluate my day until I run, have my coffee, and pray!" And though I do recommend a "morning launch," I recognize that everyone's situation is different. Find out what works best for you. This set-apart prayer time gave me a new alertness that lasted throughout my day.

Voices in the Night

One of the more intriguing things that happened after my 9/11 recommitment to prayer was what I call "voices in the night." I can't say that the voices were audible in the sense that anyone else could have heard them—my husband has not complained of hearing my "voices" at night. But each occurrence served to strengthen my faith in God's Word, bring comfort, and in some cases, move me to action. The voices reinforced my call to pray. Two episodes, with two different lessons, stand out in my mind.

Just days after the terror attacks, I had a dream so lifelike that I can still recall the images and the voice some ten years later. In the vision, I was in a low-flying aircraft looking down on a region populated with villages. I saw a huge lion prowling around, wreaking destruction wherever it went. The lion, as big as a building, would grab anything in its way and crush and shake it in its massive jaws. (No wonder Peter warned that the enemy prowls around "like a roaring lion, looking for someone to devour!") How could this horrific beast be stopped? Suddenly, a strong, quiet, but audible voice pierced my sleep with these words: "Aren't you glad you can pray for your family?" I woke up with a start, the voice still ringing in my ears.

Where did the voice come from? Was it from God? Was it something I ate the night before? I don't know, but all I can say is that it galvanized my commitment to pray. Sobered by the dream, I became much more intentional about praying for my family. I was left with the comforting assurance that prayer was a more powerful weapon than I had ever imagined.

Though I had always prayed for family and friends, my prayers were usually fueled by a crisis. No doubt I was jolted into a crisis mode in the days and weeks after 9/11. But now I was eager to find a more powerful way to pray on a daily basis—and I wanted it to be sustainable long after the crisis had died down.

Another "voice in the night" episode was a little more lighthearted than the first, but just as impactful. One morning during my Bible reading, I was reminded of how important my faith is to God. "Without faith, it's impossible to please God," the writer of Hebrews explains. "If we want to come to God," he instructs, we "must believe that He exists and that He rewards those who earnestly seek Him" (Hebrews 11:6).

I pondered and prayed about that verse, struck by the simplicity of the starting point with God: to believe that He exists and that He rewards sincere seekers. Throughout the day, I mentally repeated these words in my own loose translation: God is Real and He is a Rewarder. The Greek word for *reward,* I learned, can also mean "paycheck."

My meditation throughout the day must have sealed these words in my subconscious (which I suppose is one of the best reasons to meditate on God's words). That night, as I was in a twilight state, the same phrase kept ringing in my mind: God is Real and He is a Rewarder. . . . God is Real and He is a Rewarder. . . .

Suddenly, I was surprised in my slumber by another voice, not my own. God must have a sense of humor, because the voice I "heard" sounded like the distinctive voice of actor Morgan Freeman, whom many remember in the role of God in the movie *Bruce Almighty.* The voice interrupted my meditative strain with these words—this time in more of a roar than a whisper: "Most folks don't think I'm real."

When you get right down to it, that might be where most of us miss God in prayer. Do we really believe in the deepest part of our heart that God is real? And that He is our "Rewarder"? If so, then He has promised to respond to our faith with a "paycheck" of answered prayer. I realized that prayer and the reading of God's Word weren't meant just for devotional time. They were meant to be my life. I began to pray like it was my job.

ENLARGING MY VIEW

I continued to experiment with my prayer technique and watched for clues as to how I could pray for a world in trouble. *God, show me who is on your heart,* I would ask Him. I actually got out one of our children's globes to get a better vantage point. As our world was shaken to its core by the aftershocks of 9/11, I began to turn my eyes outward, wondering how to pray for what seemed like a very fragile planet.

I listened daily for my marching orders, remembering my analogy of the soldier, and I seemed to notice a kind of two-way communication developing between God and me. I became more sensitive to the needs all around me, which in turn, inspired more prayer. As I grew more serious about praying for the needs of my own family, I knew that God was also teaching me how to pray for His family—the world. *So how do you pray for a world in such pain?* I wondered. Maybe just one country at a time.

I explored ways to fit prayer into my busy days. Quietly, simply, I continued to pray. For family, for friends, and for the world. The Bible seemed to be the perfect field manual. I followed the instructions in 1 Timothy 2:1 to pray for "kings and all those in authority," so that we could live "peaceful and quiet lives." Peace and quiet sounded good to me amidst the turmoil surrounding the terrorist attacks.

I began looking in the newspaper and watching news reports for trouble spots in the world. I learned that if I would simply listen and be alert, God would show me where to focus my prayers. I began to pray for specific countries and even their presidents.

The children's globe made a good visual reminder to be more precise in my focus. I located suspected trouble spots. I prayed for the protection of the innocent, and especially for God's people in each nation. I prayed for those in authority—for God to change their hearts and thwart every evil attack.

My first prayer alert for a nation was sparked by a newspaper article about the Sudan. An October 11, 2001, article in the *Charlotte Observer* revealed suspicions that terrorists were being launched from Osama bin Laden's camps in Southern Sudan. Word had been leaking out for some time that this vast land, as large as the entire United States east of the Mississippi, had suffered massive genocide at the hands of the extremist government in the north. Under the radar of the world's eyes, this region was also a breeding ground for the terrible events of 9/11. This nation desperately needed prayer. So I committed to praying for the Sudan. I prayed for the suffering, for leaders, for evil to be thwarted, and especially for the persecuted followers of Christ.

As God enlarged my view, I gradually began to pray for other nations as well. News reports, Internet articles, and even casual conversations prompted prayer. No matter where I was, I found I could pause and pray. It took just about a minute to pray for a nation—I timed it. Mondays I prayed a minute for the Sudan, Tuesdays it was India, and so on.

The prayers for nations were sandwiched in between prayers for my husband and children, family and friends, neighbors—all of whom I loved "close-up." I realized quite quickly that this method was compatible with life on the go. God was reminding me to pray throughout my days, simple as that. It seemed that He was teaching me a new strategy, and while answers didn't always come when I wanted or in the way I envisioned, answers did come.

I found myself reading God's Word with an increased sense of expectancy. If I did my part to diligently seek God, the promise from His own Word was that I would be rewarded. That reward, I was to learn, included not just answered prayer but a greater awareness of God and His work all around me. This awareness spilled over into everyday life. Scripture came alive and the flywheel of prayer was turning. Prayer even became a gift I could give to others— sometimes without their ever knowing it. I began to understand what Paul meant when he talked about "praying without ceasing." This was actually becoming fun.

The Bible often links prayer with the reading of God's Word, and for good reason. God tells us that much like the rain comes down from heaven and waters the earth, yielding "seed for the sower and bread for the eater. . . . so is my word that goes out from my mouth." So I learned to "sow" the Word into the daily situations of life. Then God adds, "It will not return to me empty, but will accomplish what I desire and achieve the purpose for which I sent it" (Isaiah 55:10, 11). In time, I discovered that God's Word often had a specific word—an actual word, or maybe a phrase or an idea—just for me, if I were patient enough to search for it. I began to call that word a "watchword." I knew that God intended for me to use it in prayer.

DOUBLE FOR YOUR TROUBLE

God loves to surprise His children in much the same way we as parents love to surprise ours. As I prayed more for His world, it seemed He was increasingly active in mine.

One of my personal answered prayers still makes me smile when I think about it.

In my daily study, I was learning about how God loves to restore broken things—especially broken people. Jesus Himself quoted Isaiah's words in His first sermon. "God has sent me to preach good news to the poor . . . to bind up the broken hearted . . . and to comfort all who mourn."

Instead of their shame, God promised to give His people a double portion—"double for their trouble" (Isaiah 61:1–7). The theme of restoration after a time of suffering is one I encountered again and again. Return to your "place of safety," for there is still hope, God tells the brokenhearted children of Israel after years of captivity. He promises to repay them "two mercies for each of your troubles" (Zechariah 9:12 NLT). There it was again. God restoring double to the brokenhearted. This gave me hope as I continued to pray for hurting people and a hurting world.

During this time, Kelly, the daughter of my friend Leta, became pregnant; but several weeks into her pregnancy she was devastated when she suffered a miscarriage. I was so sad for Kelly, whom I had known since she was a child. One morning, I reflected on the words in Zechariah 9:12—"Return to your stronghold, O prisoners of hope. . . . Today I will restore to you double" (ESV). I paused for a moment, suddenly prompted to pray those words of promise for Kelly and her husband as they mourned their loss. *God loves to restore broken things*, I reminded myself. *Lord, give Kelly a double blessing to ease her pain.*

In time Kelly became pregnant again, and Leta shared the happy news. I e-mailed the verse I had been praying for her daughter out of Zechariah. Leta called and left a message. "I must talk to you, and I don't want to leave a voice mail. Please call me!"

I called, eager for more details. "You won't believe what we just learned," Leta said with a laugh. "You have been praying for Kelly to be restored double. This week, we learned she is having twins." Though I was just one of many who prayed, I felt like I had been given a front-row seat to God's special miracle.

Kelly and her husband, Jason, rejoiced together about the goodness of God and His character as a "double blesser." Now little

Kanah and Grace are daily reminders for them of how God loves to restore double for your trouble. Just for fun and as a constant reminder for me, I ordered my first personalized license plate for my little Volkswagen: RESTORE2.

Ten years later, with much practice and learning under my belt, I have seen countless answers to specific prayers, both small and large. My circle of close friends now extends beyond the suburbs, stretching from inner-city Charlotte neighborhoods to genocide-torn villages in Africa.

I am astounded when I think of the ways God has answered some of my "globe-sweeping" prayers. I am also amazed as I've watched Him intervene in the personal lives of those I love. The secret, I believe, is in the asking, in the listening. In being alert. Sometimes God whispers, sometimes He roars. I am learning to hear the voice of my Father.

Chapter 2

Keep Watch

Devote yourselves to prayer, being watchful and thankful.

—COLOSSIANS 4:2

Most anyone gets excited by the shiny and drama-filled moments of life, moments when God seems to shout, rather than whisper. When our three children were young, we traveled through southern Africa one summer as invited guests of our dear friends Bryan and June. They were our companions and guides during this once-in-a-lifetime experience for our family. The former South African residents had never lost their love for their homeland, nor did their sense of breathless wonder disappear.

BG and Auntie June, as our children affectionately called them, introduced us to the adventure of safari in the African bush. They rejoiced with us over our big-game sightings: the elephant herd, a giraffe family feeding on tree leaves, a rhino charging, a spitting cobra, or some lions on the prowl.

But their greatest moments of glee came when we happened upon the subtleties that most people would miss. Their trained and watchful eyes guided our children to carefully notice more than 120 bird species. We witnessed an air battle between two birds of prey amid BG's shouts of surprise. June bubbled with amazement over the sight of two rare dwarf mongooses rearing their tiny heads out of their burrows after a sudden rain shower. Our family became more watchful, more thankful, and more amazed during our trip. We had learned to notice the small things and our eyes were rewarded by unexpected treasures.

Surely I could find a way to apply this same watchfulness to prayer. I was beginning to see watching as an important aspect of being alert, so I hoped to find practical examples. I was intrigued to learn that Methodist founder John Wesley also understood the importance of watching for God and even instructed his early followers to practice what he called the "discipline of watching" God at work on a daily basis.

I soon realized that if I noticed God at work only when I saw the "big-game" moments, I would spend most of my waking moments slightly disappointed, thirsty, thankless. But when I was really watching, I would often be amazed by the subtle things. Little "dwarf mongooses" of answered prayer began to appear in the most unexpected places. A friend I hadn't seen in years might cross my mind, so I would pray. Later, I might encounter her during an unplanned trip to the store. A child would pass a difficult exam with flying colors. I would suddenly remember that I had prayed. Maybe the answer came in the form of a breakthrough in a long-standing problem. Or extra income would come from an unexpected source. Tiny miracles on a daily basis made me wonder, *How many answers to prayers have I missed over the years simply because I wasn't watching?*

Half the battle seemed to be in remembering the things I prayed for during my morning prayer time. Answers would practically smack me in the face, reminding me, *Oh yeah, I prayed about that.*

You would think that having a daily audience with the Creator of the Universe would be enough to make anyone's heart beat fast. But somehow I found the sheer ordinariness of prayer to be its own undoing. It was so easy to let prayer become stale or fall into neglect and disrepair in the daily absence of "big moments," once the initial crisis of 9/11 had passed. But I wanted my prayer for the world to be sustainable. I wanted to stay alert, to keep listening for God's whispers. Daily.

As I've shared, I was already learning important lessons on alertness from the book of 1 Peter. I remembered that he was encouraging a persecuted church to be "self-controlled and alert" for the purpose of effective prayer. These words were first written in Koine Greek, the language of the day. *Alertness* (*sophroneo,* from "saved" and "mind") means "sober-minded" or "self-disciplined"; *self-control (enkrateia)* means "with strength or power." This sounded more like instructions to athletes than lessons in prayer.

It's no wonder Paul compares prayer and the building of one's faith to a battle. He admonishes us to "fight the fight of faith." Over and over we are reminded that this earth is still crawling with enemies—seen and unseen. And like I've said, after 9/11 my commitment to pray was my way of signing up for combat duty. It's not surprising that I would discover that becoming disciplined for the purpose of prayer would be a bit like boot camp!

I was further encouraged when I discovered that another word in the Bible for alertness is *watchfulness.* The Apostle Paul encouraged the believers not to be like those who are "asleep," but to be "alert and self-controlled" (1 Thessalonians 5:6). The word for *alert* here can actually be translated as "to keep watch."

Jesus Himself warned His closest circle of disciples to keep watch. "Watch and pray so you don't fall into temptation," He told the sleepy disciples in the Garden of Gethsemane. "Watch out for false teachers, those wolves in sheep's clothing," He cautioned. "Watch out for greed," and above all, "Keep watch for my return." Seems like part of the daily life of anyone who wants to follow Christ is being watchful.

PRAYER TRIGGERS

At its most basic, staying connected to God in prayer is simply remembering to pray—and then remembering to watch for answers. I have found there are practical ways to sharpen the skill of remembering and have learned to weave reminders to pray into my ordinary days. The best trick I discovered for keeping watch are "prayer triggers." During our years of infertility, for some reason I adopted bunnies as my symbol of hope that God could do a miracle. Though I held tightly to God's Word, discouragement would loom at times like a dark cloud. Bunnies would often appear at the precise moment our hopes were ready to be dashed. Even my big six-foot-seven husband grew attached to our little "bunny trigger."

In a lighthearted though powerful way, these bunnies often encouraged our dream to have a child. Friends learned our little secret, and sometimes gave bunnies as gifts during our years of waiting. Then more bunnies of celebration came after our babies were born—cards, figurines, prints, an oil painting, even a handsome antique English stone sculpture. Our kids once decided to count the bunnies—subtle and not so subtle—sprinkled throughout our home. I think they lost count at a hundred.

The Bible is full of examples of visual reminders. I think of the "stones of remembrance" that the patriarchs erected to remind themselves of God's victories and answered prayer. Even the New Testament word for *sign* can mean "signal, symbol, or finger-mark."

God seems to constantly leave "fingerprints," or reminders for His people to watch and pray and trust Him.

I mentioned that right after 9/11, I found the children's globe to be a good reminder to pray for the world. There were other prayer triggers for various places on my heart for prayer—a dress hanging in my closet from a Pakistani friend often nudged me to pray for her country. Numerous artifacts from my African travels reminded me to pray for God's people in the Sudan, Rwanda, Burundi, Ethiopia. Sprinkled throughout my day were reminders to pray.

My friend Lisa took the prayer trigger idea to a new level. At the time she was leading the small-group Bible study to which I belonged. A true encourager, she loves teamwork. Lisa is also passionate to find practical ways to help women grow in their faith. She encouraged each woman in our group to select her own prayer trigger to remind us to pray for one another during the day.

For instance, Lisa's trigger is "anything leopard." If I go shopping, I'm certain to run across leopard print on at least one item. Diana loves teapots, Sally picked redbirds, Tonya's triggers are red cars, Jacqui's are orchids; Marcela, our "audio learner," selected singing birds. You get the point.

The interesting thing is that on any given day, several prayer triggers for our group, which numbers more than a dozen, will cross my path. So daily life is sprinkled with reminders to pray for my friends. I'm beginning to assign triggers to other friends and family members. The neat thing is that there seems to be no limit—there is always room in my memory bank for just one more trigger.

WATCHWORDS

I was always on the lookout for other secrets to help me become more watchful and alert. One of the more remarkable things I had noticed when I turned my life over to Christ years ago was that instead of being a dead book, as I previously thought, the Bible came alive for me.

From experience, I had discovered that God's Word often had a word—a verse, a phrase, a concept, or an actual word—just for me, if I was patient enough to search for it. I called them my "watchwords." During my days of struggling with infertility, I would often find a personal watchword of encouragement. Other times, God's Word would give me wisdom. And somehow, almost mysteriously, it always strengthened my faith. Paul tells us in Romans 10:17 that faith actually comes by "hearing the Word of God."

I knew God intended for me to use His Word in prayer. My friend Helen helped the concept of watchwords come alive for me when she described how she prayed for her children. She and her husband had raised their children in Africa while serving as missionaries. "When I was faced with situations that seemed impossible," she shared, "I was reminded of David's battles with the giant Goliath. I would hold on to one verse of Scripture—my one smooth stone— and trust God would provide just what I needed for my victory." We'll discuss more about the importance of watchwords later. For now, it helps to remember that scripture can be part of watching for signs of God's work in your life.

My continued efforts to pray using my watchwords only heightened my watchfulness. This, in turn, increased my alertness to God's voice. As my inner hearing got better and my eyes were more watchful, my prayers grew even more precise in nature.

PRECISION PRAYERS

And precision, as I've shared earlier, is important in spiritual as well as earthly battles. A turning point in World War II weapon technology was the development of precision bombing. Through a somewhat crude forerunner of the Global Positioning System (GPS), precision bombing enabled the United States to focus on bombing German military sites, and especially artillery arsenals, decreasing the civilian casualties.

I once heard the story of a young bomber pilot who wrote to his family, "I consider myself a pacifist. Nothing in me wants to harm the German people. But when I remember Hitler and the horror inflicted by the Nazis, I am compelled to destroy the evil." Precision bombing allowed our fighter pilots to focus their attack on the enemy and, as much as possible, avoid the innocent.

Despite fears of another terrorist attack after 9/11, I discovered that somehow it just didn't feel right to pray for God to "destroy all our enemies." We didn't know who was innocent, or initially, even the source of the threats. I found it helpful to read my Bible, meditate on its message, and ask God for wisdom on how to pray with greater precision for a nation and world at war.

I was compelled to pray for the protection of our nation and its leaders, our borders, our states, our city, home, neighbors, and especially our troops—several by name. I prayed daily for God to guard us. I also wanted (and still want) evil to be defeated.

Our children's globe continued to be a good prayer trigger, or visual reminder, to be more precise in my prayer focus. So I located suspected trouble spots. I began to pray for Afghanistan, Iraq, Pakistan, Sudan, and other areas suspected to harbor terrorists. I prayed for the protection of the innocent civilians, and especially for God's people in each area. I prayed for those in authority—for God to change hearts, where necessary, and to thwart every attack.

It might be good to pause a minute here to emphasize God's heart for the whole world. The promise from John 3:16 is clear:

"For God so loved the world that he gave his one and only Son, that whoever believes in him will not perish but have eternal life." Salvation is for anyone, anywhere in the world, just for the asking. God has no geographical favorites. But when evil men choose to inflict hatred and violence on the innocent, especially children, God speaks with more of a roar than a whisper.

I thought about the thousands of American men, women, and children who perished in the World Trade Center attacks and how deeply our nation was grieving for her people. I also became increasingly aware of the thousands of innocent people who had suffered at the hands of their own governments. I felt compelled to pray for God's hand of protection and justice.

During the months after 9/11, numbers of human rights reports surfaced about the Saddam Hussein regime in Iraq. Up to 150,000 Iraqi dissidents and Shia Muslims are estimated to have been tortured and killed during his reign from 1979 to 2003. Most horrific had been the 1987 genocide in which Hussein forces mounted a torture-and-attack campaign against the Kurds, killing nearly 200,000 of his own citizens. Men, women, babies, and the elderly were brutally murdered, their bodies discovered in mass graves.

But how should I pray? It was overwhelming. I asked God for wisdom from His Word. I had long been using a daily Bible reading plan.[1] Each morning the Word of God seemed to give both passion and precision to my prayers. Psalm 55 happened to be the selected reading for September 11. When I stopped on verse 9, I sensed the Lord's voice telling me that this was to be my "precision" prayer: "Confuse the wicked, O Lord, confound their speech, for I see violence and strife in the city." I began to pray that the enemy's speech would be confused, and even that their tongues would turn on one another. I learned that throughout the Old Testament, God often chose to defeat enemies in this manner.

Some time later I stumbled upon God's Words through the prophet Isaiah (chapter 59:4–7). He utterly condemns the actions of evil and violent oppressors, comparing them to spiders. "They speak lies, conceive trouble, give birth to evil . . . they spin a spider's web . . . acts of violence are in their hands and their feet rush into sin . . . they are swift to shed innocent blood." Somehow it helped to pray these verses fervently for the overthrow of Hussein. I continued to pray for the enemy's "speech to be confused," and for "tongues to turn on one another." While I didn't pray for his death, I did pray earnestly for his capture.

Days later international news broke of Saddam Hussein's capture. On a December morning in 2003, I was both relieved and intrigued to learn that Iraqi informants had turned against their own leaders. Their tongues had indeed "turned on one another." By locating exactly where Hussein was hiding, our special forces eliminated the danger of loss of innocent life. The brave informants were instrumental in helping U.S. forces in the gathering of intelligence that led our forces right to Hussein's hiding place in a remote, underground dugout. News reports referred to this hideout, of all things, as "a spider hole." I know many around the world were compelled to pray; this miracle was not accomplished by my prayers alone. But I felt as if I were part of a large chorus of people crying out in prayer to God for help. And I believe, because God had begun to help me be alert and watchful, I got a glimpse of the answer.

THANKFULNESS

More reinforcement in my new habit of watchfulness came from a surprising corner. I began to realize that good old-fashioned gratitude, when I expressed it, sharpened my spiritual eyes and made me more alert to answers that might have otherwise gone unnoticed. When I took time to be thankful, it was as if my eyes were opened to even more of God's work around me. I'm not sure why this is so—perhaps it was because I slowed down and took time to actually notice the evidence of God's intervention. Paul also knew this to be true, and reminds his readers in Colossians 4:2 to be "thankful" as well as "watchful" in prayer.

Gratitude, I would learn, is a powerful ingredient in keeping us alert for prayer. "Enter his gates with thanksgiving and his courts with praise," David wrote in Psalm 100, known the world over as a recipe for praise. There is even more about the exercise of praise and thanksgiving in the Bible than prayer.

However, I notice that when things come too easily, I have this twisted tendency to be less thankful for my blessings. Abundance can make us numb. Take water, for example. Except under drought conditions, water is one of life's blessings that is most accessible to me on a daily basis. I usually drink it, bathe in it, wash clothes and dishes with it, waste it—all without much thought.

Yet, in a recent trip to the Sudan, life revolved around the daily search for this treasure called water. In starkly short supply, water is quite literally the difference between life and death in the bush. In 120-degree heat, one is humbled by the dependency on this life-giving substance—always watching for opportunities to drink it, and desperately thankful for its supply.

After 9/11 I realized I had taken so many things for granted—my freedom, my faith, the safety of my family. What could I do to enhance my sense of gratitude? How could I develop true thankfulness?

For starters, I found that if I could manage to slow down my pace a bit, this made me better able to watch—and be more alert to my blessings. Things that I might have taken for granted started to catch my interest. I found myself focusing more on the faces of my children when I talked to them, pausing to really look into their eyes. How beautiful those eyes were, and how seldom I took the time to drink in their wonder.

Same with other everyday blessings. I reflected on the many ways my husband took the time to speak encouraging words to me—many men don't speak that language—and how thankful I was that he knew just what to say to me and when. Perhaps I stopped now and then to savor a newly painted room or to listen to the night sounds in our backyard. Was everything becoming more wondrous or was I just tuned in?

I even noticed a lifting in my overall mood. As a side note, I have found that my mental and physical health seem to improve in tandem with this developing "sense of wonder" that accompanies thankfulness. Apparently these "feel-good" responses have a physiological basis. Researchers studied subjects who practiced sustained gratitude for just five minutes and found that they experienced a rise in the level of disease-fighting antibodies that lasted several hours.

I was also inspired to become more thankful by the teenage daughter of a friend. Molly discovered a way to practice "sustained gratitude" by writing in what she called her "thank-you book" each day. She found it difficult to think of even a few things to write in her book at first, but her daily list eventually numbered in the hundreds as she began watching more closely for signs of God at work. Friends and family marveled as Molly changed from a somewhat depressed teenager to one whose faith and joyful attitude inspired all who knew her. Right out of college, she chose to spend a couple of years as a missionary, sharing her love of God in Spain.

As I noticed more and more answers to prayer, I began to stop and savor the moment, thanking God. Pray. Listen. Watch. Give thanks. This practice of gratitude, like the follow-through on a proper golf or tennis swing, seemed to complete the process of staying alert.

I kept listening for God's whispers and watching for signs of His work all around me. My faith grew as I noticed more answers to my prayers. I trusted God more in the daily details because I had seen Him in action.

Prayer is also more organic than most people think. Raw honesty with God, combined with a surrendered heart, invites Him into our real-life situations. As I continued to remind God that I was available to pray for His world, I became increasingly alert to what was happening in the world beyond my own walls. I might read about a terrorist attack in India or the persecution of believers in China. An Internet article about human suffering would catch my eye. I would pray briefly about the need. Often I would become alert to further mention of the need, and thus be reminded to pray— quietly, simply, again and again.

Day-to-day living took on new vibrancy as watchful prayer made me more attuned to the human suffering along my path. I would strike up a conversation with a young mother in the grocery store, only to find she was a victim of domestic violence. In the Phoenix airport I sat next to a young soldier named Jesse. He was headed for Alaska, and then on to Afghanistan. I promised him I'd pray, and now "Soldier Jesse" has a spot on my prayer list. Were there more people in pain or was I just seeing the world through new eyes?

Most surprising about my new commitment to alertness in prayer was a dramatic decrease in my tendency to fear and worry. This was a big relief since I had wrestled with these twin "demons" for most of my life. However, I found it interesting that my anxieties didn't simply drop off, but rather gave fuel for my prayer. And I could never have imagined that fear and worry would actually provide the raw material for my next big breakthrough in prayer, my discovery of the list.

PART TWO

Be Specific

Chapter 3

The List

In the morning, O LORD, You will hear my voice;
In the morning I will order my prayer to You and eagerly watch.

—PSALM 5:3, NASB

I didn't have to learn how to worry. It just came naturally as a by-product of an overactive imagination, a curious mind, and a relentless memory. Marriage and a family only brought more responsibility, and therefore more things to worry about. I agree with my friend who defines worry with the acronym W.O.R.R.Y.: Worry Only Robs Rest from You. It's true. Worry is exhausting. It sure took a lot of my energy to worry. There's an old Revolutionary War saying that goes something like this: "If you have to choose between alertness and anxiety in battle, choose to be alert. You will stay alive a whole lot longer."

Since my decision to follow Christ years earlier, I had a history of seeing God work. I knew He could be trusted. But when trouble or crisis would hit, I was tempted to jump back into my old patterns. During this prayer journey, originally sparked by the fear surrounding 9/11, I was determined to put anxiety to flight. Perhaps there was a way to make the furious energy of anxiety work for me instead of against me.

MAKING ANXIETY WORK FOR ME

I was inspired by Paul's letter to some persecuted Christians in Philippi. They were always in danger of getting killed, and therefore had lots to worry about. "Don't worry about anything," he encouraged them. "Instead, pray about everything." I was struck by the word *instead*. Paul didn't just stay stop worrying. He said, instead of worrying, pray. It seemed to me like he was saying to redirect the energy of worry into prayer.

I understood that concept. It sounded a little like a trick I had learned back in high school when I took karate in between my sports seasons. I was taught to use the enemy's energy against him. A violent attack could be redirected to incapacitate my attacker. The Bible reminds us that we are in a spiritual battle. "Tell God what you need and thank Him for all He has done," Paul says. "If you do this, you will experience God's peace, which is far more wonderful than the human mind can understand. His peace will guard your hearts and minds as you live in Christ Jesus" (Philippians 4:6, 7 NLT). Some versions of the Bible use the word *petition* for prayer requests instead of the word *need*. Petition can be defined as "a request for particular benefits." This sounded like a list to me. What better way to disarm the powers of darkness, I reasoned, than to turn the very anxiety intended to disable us into energy for a powerful counterattack? My tendency to worry became the very thing that inspired my list. And it sounded to me like Paul was saying that listing my concerns was a pathway to pursuing God's peace.

When you love people, worry comes with the territory. I keep telling myself that if I didn't love, I would have very little to worry about. So I spend a lot of time in prayer. But does prayer really work in the war against worry? Simply praying won't overcome worry unless we can trust that God actually has the answers to the things that cause us concern. I want my prayers to work. And how could I know whether answers came unless I was watching for them? I needed to become more specific in my prayers.

So my worry list became a prayer list of sorts, or as nineteenth-century preacher Charles Spurgeon admonished, I turned my "cares into prayers."[1] Thus began the list.

I should confess to you that I love lists. A list helps to streamline the information that passes daily into my brain. I can't resist the urge to find out about the "top ten super foods," or "five ways to strengthen your marriage," or "seven simple secrets I wish I had known about parenting when I first had kids." My prayer list functions in much the same way. As I am surrounded by the flood of concerns daily, the list gives me better aim.

There's a temptation, however, to take lists to the extreme. A list of requests can quickly become a tool for control and a source of much angst and frustration if we're not careful. Conscious of that pitfall, I sought to find a way to make the list my friend—a gentle but effective means of sharpening my prayer requests. This, in turn, helped me to be alert and watch for answers on a daily basis. And as I kept learning, seeing God's answers further increased my faith, which in turn kicked out worry. Beyond that, I found that the list became a reminder, kind of a "memorial stone" of God's work all around me (Joshua 4:6, 7).

MAKING MY LIST

To form my list, I started by simply writing down every family member, friend, co-worker, situation, problem, or place that somehow grabbed my heart. With friends and family, it was pretty obvious. But then I began to think about certain goals or dreams and those of my husband and children. I moved on to my problem areas, faults and weaknesses, persistent worries. Then I took a look at the world around me, beginning with my neighborhood and community, and moving outward to the world beyond my own sphere of concerns. This took some time for reflection.

Initially, my list grew to about fifty items. I knew that I couldn't maintain a prayer list of fifty requests per day, so I decided to number each item from one to seven, and then I began praying for each need on the corresponding day of the week. For instance, I prayed for all number ones on Monday. My Monday list included my husband, my dad, the nation of Sudan, the Furrs (missionaries in France), our sons' athletic coaches, and wisdom in simplifying my schedule and home, to name a few. The list began to grow. Eventually I would also add a few "POD" prayers each day, or "prayers on demand," since there was always a pressing need for someone. Things would daily cross my path for prayer that were not on my list, so I knew I had to allow the flexibility to pray for urgent needs as they arose.

I also concluded that a prayer list seemed much less like drudgery if I didn't have to rush through it. If I carved out the time—which was just after my run—the unhurried quiet, along with a fresh cup of coffee before my family arose, made "listening" a little more peaceful and my heart more responsive.

Plus, with a list, my prayers were easier to remember. Prayer could easily accompany chores, and dead time became a chance to pray. If I couldn't think of a specific prayer for someone, I would borrow a tip from John DeVries, founder of Mission India, from his book *Why Pray?*[2] I'd ask God to "B.L.E.S.S." those on the list: I prayed for their Body, their Labor, their Emotional health, their

Social relationships, and their Spiritual life in Christ. With the list, prayers gained traction and answers seemed to pop up in subtle ways.

DAILY THEMES

How specific should we be when praying? After some thought, I decided that prayer should be specific enough that I would recognize an answer when it came. I discovered that a lot of vagueness in my prayers occurs when I'm just too lazy to take the time to consider what God might be asking me to pray in a particular situation or what I am asking God to do—give me wisdom, provide for a need, open a door, help me overcome a temptation, or solve a problem.

George Mueller, a nineteenth-century pioneer in prayer, is a great example of how specificity in prayer can move mountains. He wrote about how he "mined" the Word daily and found food for the soul and promises to hang on to, which fueled and energized his prayers, creating a pattern that sustained his work for decades and gave birth to legendary answers to prayer. Mueller founded a vast empire of orphanages throughout England, without any fundraising methods . . . other than prayer.

I loved Mueller's advice, and it was very nice to have a structured prayer list, but I felt there was something missing. I was intrigued by the prayer method outlined by John DeVries in *Why Pray?* He shares practical tips on specific and strategic prayer and its amazing impact on the work of Mission India. Years earlier, my husband had spent three weeks traveling with John and his team, witnessing firsthand the miracles they encountered. We have been praying for India and investing in their ministry ever since. India has a billion people—it is home to one out of every six people on earth. Nearly half of those have never even heard the *name* of Jesus. Sharing the Gospel and planting churches in the remote or even hostile areas of India was difficult and dangerous work. Mission India workers saw doors miraculously open when these areas had first been prepared with prayer.

Inspired by this approach, I created a strategy, incorporating a different attribute of God as a prayer theme for each day of the week. What good would praying specifically do if I didn't even acknowledge God's character and power to influence our world? This method proved to be a good framework for my list. Here are the themes I used for each day of the week:

Mondays: Pray for God to Prohibit Evil.
Tuesdays: Pray for God's Provision.
Wednesdays: Pray for God's Miracle-Working Power.
Thursdays: Pray for God's Problem-Solving Wisdom.
Fridays: Pray for God's Presence.
Saturdays: Pray for God's Purpose.
Sundays: Praise God for His Goodness.

Surely this would help me to increase the scope of my prayers. I applied this strategy to praying both for my own personal needs and for nations. Over time, I found that using this format helped me to shape the prayers for each day.

I need to stress how simple this format is. Remember, I am like most busy people, trying to balance family, work, and the countless demands of ministry. The framework became part of my daily thinking, which added structure and clarity to my days, not more burdens!

And as I grew more comfortable with my list and daily themes, I became increasingly sensitive to God's voice. When my husband, David, calls, he doesn't have to identify himself. I immediately recognize his voice. That's how it began to feel with God when I added praying through these attributes to my daily routine. The routine was fine-tuning my ability to have a clearer eye for God's work and a keener ear for His voice.

I also began to notice that God's attributes came to life for me. I began to see Him more and more as my Provider, my source of wisdom, the giver of my purpose in life. I even noticed that prayers were answered, sometimes on days that I had prayed for that particular attribute.

DIVINE INTERSECTIONS

More and more, the list was becoming linked to my life. A name or a face would come to mind on a given day, without my even having to look at my list.

For example, I remember reflecting on my Wednesday list one day, noticing that I had been praying for Nancy, my friend from Vietnam for whom I had prayed to know Christ. I hadn't seen Nancy in a couple of years. That particular Wednesday, as I headed into a grocery store I rarely frequented, I asked God if I should still keep praying for Nancy.

Seconds later, I turned the corner and practically bumped into her husband. He told me Nancy's whereabouts and I was able to reconnect with her that week. I took that as a pretty clear sign to keep praying specifically for the Lord to reveal His love to Nancy and her family. Answers like this appeared quietly as I was on the lookout. My husband called them "divine intersections." The psalmist's words resonated with me: "Listen to my voice in the morning, LORD. Each morning I bring my requests to you and wait expectantly" (Psalm 5:3, NLT). Morning after morning, I would make my list and "keep watch" for the answers (Psalm 5:3, ASV).

Here's another example: Thursdays included prayers for China. I began to feel like I knew a Chinese pastor I prayed for named Sam Lamb. Reverend Lamb was mentioned among persecuted Christians worldwide during the International Day of Prayer for the Persecuted Church back in November of 2003. In prison for years, he simply prayed for "revival, strength, and fruit." So I added him to my Thursday list. In addition to praying for God's problem-solving wisdom, I also prayed for the nation of China, for Sam Lamb, and for "revival, strength, and fruit."

One evening, the rest of the family was at a football game and I chose to stay home. I can't remember why, but I was feeling rather weary and discouraged. I remember praying a feeble prayer, *God, I really need to know You are here with me—that You are listening. I don't even have the strength to seek You very hard right now.* I happened to glance over at a stack of my husband's books and magazines. There among the pile was a copy of the magazine *Christian History*, not exactly light reading. Why I prayed the next prayer, I can't say, but it was rather audacious looking back. *And by the way, God, I am going to pick up the driest-looking magazine of the bunch. Even You probably can't find a way to lift my spirits with* Christian History.

Now if I hadn't been so weary, I might have been a little more careful about throwing down a gauntlet to the living God. Settling back against my bed pillows, I began to mindlessly flip through the magazine, which happened to feature a story about the prolific house church phenomenon in Communist China. Thought by some to be among the largest collection of Christians on the globe, the heavily persecuted house church movement may number in the tens of millions.

Inspiring, I thought, rather lamely. *But God, after all these years of praying for China, I wish You would give me a glimpse of Sam Lamb.* I will never forget turning the page, and for a freeze-framed moment in time, I looked at the smiling face in the photograph staring back at me. What was it about that face? Surely not. . . . I caught my breath, not daring to look at the caption. And then—I looked down to see the name, Reverend Samuel Lamb! After being imprisoned for more than twenty years, he was released as a pastor to a church of more than two thousand. I learned that Reverend Lamb is one of China's most courageous and influential Christians.[3] Astounding. *Will I ever actually meet Sam Lamb?* I wondered. Maybe not until heaven, but I have a greater awareness of and sense of prayer partnership with persecuted Christian brothers and sisters in China. And I'm grateful to God for giving me a look at the courageous man for whom I'd prayed. Sam Lamb's name and his face are indelibly etched on my heart—and my prayer list.

THE LIST COMES ALIVE

Strangely enough, the list began to take on a life of its own. As I focused on certain people and places each day, I grew to feel somewhat connected to them. Of course it's not surprising that I would feel close to David every day of the week. After all, he is my husband. But on the days I specifically prayed for him, I seemed to be especially sensitive to his needs. That made sense to me. But what surprised me was that over time, my bond with places like the Sudan began to grow as well.

I had initially felt nudged to pray for the Sudan when reading the article in our city's paper on the heels of 9/11. From that point on, I seemed to often stumble on reports about the Sudan on the radio, television, everywhere I went. Christians and eventually even Black African Muslims were targeted. This horrific genocide lasted over two decades, slaughtered more than two million citizens, and displaced more than twice that many.

I began to feel an urgent sense to pray for the nation of Sudan. An excerpt from my journal dated October 11, 2001, reads:

> Confession: Lord, I have not prayed and travailed for the suffering of Your people worldwide. My view has been so narrow. The great suffering among Your people in the Sudan is staggering. Show me how to pray, Lord.

The situation was urgent and I had committed to pray for the Sudan every Monday. But eventually Monday's prayer for the Sudan began to feel hollow. How could I get my arms around such a huge nation with enormous needs? Again, I wondered, *Can the prayers of one person really make a difference?* One night I caught part of a Sudan documentary and was struck by the plight of so many refugees returning home after a fragile Comprehensive Peace Agreement was signed in 2005. Watching the tragic story of a man wandering in search of his family, I decided I would pray for that man. I called him "Sudan Sam" and prayed that somehow he would be reconnected with his family. From then on the Sudan had a face. I prayed for a "Sudan Sam," whoever and wherever he was.

Every Monday, for about a minute, there was the Sudan and especially "Sudan Sam" on my heart in prayer. To my surprise, a door eventually opened for me to travel to Southern Sudan. David, who had a broadcast background and had filled in as an occasional anchor, had been asked by our community's largest talk radio station, WBT, to do what they called "A Moment of Hope" for their stunned listening audience during the days and weeks that followed 9/11.

The popular minute of inspiration each morning had become a regular feature, as had his *David Chadwick Show*. During his "Moment of Hope" in the fall of 2007, David invited the city of

Charlotte to take action to help Darfur, a region in western Sudan as big as Texas. Its mostly Muslim, black African inhabitants had recently suffered the same kind of horrific genocide that the citizens of Southern Sudan had endured for years at the hands of the Islamic extremist Arab North. This time, however, the world was watching. Even celebrities joined in the campaign to "Save Darfur."

The morning broadcast personalities from WBT Radio, Al Gardner and Stacey Simms, city favorites, had joined with David to encourage our city to donate to Sacks of Hope, relief kits to be distributed there. The nearly half-million dollars that was collected purchased these relief kits, which were assembled by Christian Solidarity International (CSI), a group working against human rights violations in the Sudan, including the practice of human trafficking.

In the spring of 2008, we were on our way! As our DC-3 took off from the humanitarian aid compound on the Kenya border, I looked out on the parched plains of Southern Sudan. Our team of twelve consisted of several members of our church in Charlotte, a top-level Samaritan's Purse leader, a Christian Solidarity International worker, and two documentary filmmakers from our local news station.

A few minutes after takeoff, I began to feel uneasy. We were flying too low. We should have reached our cruising altitude by then. *Something is wrong!* I thought. Sure enough, the pilot informed us that our plane was having trouble. He circled back and made an emergency landing on the dusty Kenyan runway. The part needed for the plane's repair would be delivered by van, so we waited for six hours in the stifling sub-Saharan heat. The part arrived, but further attempts to repair the plane failed, so we departed the next morning, leaving behind the DC-3 and continuing our long journey in two small Cessna Caravans.

We delivered the relief kits to a group of women and children near Darfur who had just fled the cruel militia forces known as *Janjaweed* ("devils on horseback"); they had left barefoot in the middle of the night for a two-day journey on foot.

Our two small Cessnas then made the long journey to a remote area in the Nuba Mountains, where we spent days with a group of Samaritan's Purse workers. Franklin Graham, president of this international aid group, had briefed us before the journey. More than eight hundred churches, he informed us, had been utterly destroyed by the extremist Islamic government based in the Northern Sudanese city of Khartoum. Often they were burned with worshipers inside.

The Nuba Mountain region, near the border of North and South Sudan, had been hit especially hard by the war. Pastors told us of the rape and torture of many Christians. Some were even crucified. Entire villages were destroyed. And for more than two decades, the eyes of the world were elsewhere.

For Graham, the rebuilding of churches in Southern Sudan had become his master passion. If the villagers saw their places of worship restored, Franklin said, they would have hope and courage to rebuild their land. It was a tangible way to communicate the worldwide support of the Christian community to these persecuted people.

At that point Samaritan's Purse had completed about two hundred churches. By 2011 they had rebuilt more than four hundred churches and were fully committed to their mission to restore all eight hundred churches! Graham had also recruited energetic teams of young men and women from all over the United States and Canada to work on the construction of a Bible college for Sudanese pastors.

While in the Nuba Mountain region, David and I grew fond of Zaki, our Sudanese interpreter. A survivor of the brutal war, this joyful man was the son of the first convert to Christianity in that region. His clipped British accent gave a clue to some years of schooling in England. He had returned in 2005 to head up the church-rebuilding efforts with Samaritan's Purse.

One evening during a time of group sharing, I mentioned that I had been praying for the Sudan for seven years and had even nicknamed someone "Sudan Sam."

Zaki look startled and blurted, "That's me! I am Sudan Sam! My name is Zaki Samwiil" (Arabic for Samuel). "My father was also Samuel. There's even a book about his life called *Samwiil of Sudan!*"[4] Zaki and I practically laughed and cried at the same time as he realized that my prayers for "Sudan Sam" to find his family were probably most intense during the time he was making the difficult transition from England back to his homeland and his people in the Nuba Mountains. We were amazed that our lives had been connected by a nudge to pray for a nation.

I reflected on the odds against such an unlikely encounter, and for a moment, the earth seemed very small. "Zaki," I said quietly, "can you believe that halfway around the world, God alerted me to pray for you by name before I ever knew you?" I knew what it meant: God loved both of us very much.

My list continued to grow within my own small world. Family, friends, and even perfect strangers began to ask for prayer. There was Anna, whose son Robert was leaving for Iraq. A couple struggling with infertility wanted prayer. A mechanic who had helped us when we had car trouble would not let us pay him but asked if I would pray that he would find a wife. All these people made my list. Tuesday was the day I prayed for special blessings for my mother.

Wednesdays I prayed for my sister Susan. David's brother, Howard, and his wife, Ramona, were on Friday's list. A dear friend longing to receive custody of the foster baby she'd cared for since birth was on Saturday.

The various needs on my list for each day became part of my daily pattern. Eventually, even my unconscious thought processes seemed to cooperate with my list. I would realize at some point in my day, maybe while making one of my boring drives across town, *It's Tuesday, God. That means I am trusting You as my Provider today. And Tuesday means India. Be with my running buddy Susan, who leaves for a medical missions trip to India next month. It's also the day to pray for our daughter. Please continue to give her strength and wisdom.* Ordinary days no longer felt ordinary.

You have your own world of concerns that are different from mine. You may be facing perplexing situations with your family—burdens that quietly weigh you down. And I imagine your heart for the world is also different—you may never set foot in Africa. But I hope the concept of pouring your heart out to God in the form of a specific list will help to build your faith.

You will have an opportunity in the following chapter to make your own list. Even if you are not a list maker by nature, I hope you will at least walk through the process. Modify the list to fit your schedule and personality. Regardless of what form your list ends up taking, I think you'll find it helps to sharpen your spiritual listening and watching and that it brings focus to your prayers. And as you list the things that you hold most dear, I hope you will be more alert to watching God at work in your own life in both big and small ways. I trust that this process will help you to build your faith and kick out fear.

Chapter 4

The Chubby Book Method

Teach us to number our days, . . . that we may gain a heart of wisdom.

—Psalm 90:12

I imagine that by now, you are already thinking about the people and places you want to pray for—the cares that burden your own heart. I'll walk you through the same steps I took so you can make your own list.

We've talked about the importance of staying alert and ready for prayer throughout the day. Listening and watching are key. It's also important to be specific—finding "watchwords" in the Bible helps you focus your prayers and notice answers. The daily themes I've shared with you encourage you to focus on God Himself. We're developing a relationship here, not a business transaction.

I found an easy way to bring all these pieces together using a simple item you can pick up at any office supply store—a small wire-bound book of note cards. I call this the "Chubby Book." I've kept journals for years and have used countless Bible study formats. But the Chubby Book remains a constant for me. We'll use the

Chubby Book to bring all the moving parts of this prayer process together. But first, take some time to make your list.

Raw Material for Prayer

Before you write down anything, it helps to take stock of your life. When you make your list, you will have a chance to turn your "cares into prayers." Many of our worries revolve around those we love deeply. Some people find they experience a bit of relief simply by writing down the worries on paper. No need is too big or too small. Remember throughout this process that "nothing is impossible for God."

When making your list, don't forget that your hopes and dreams are also important. In fact, I found that some of my dreams were so close to my heart, they could only be shared with God. Every time I looked at my list, I remembered to dream big. Perplexing problems, areas for personal growth, anywhere I needed God's help made my list. Worries, hopes, dreams, problems, people whom I loved were no longer just issues. They became the raw materials for prayer. The list provided a way to jump-start my prayer each morning. Then the spontaneous "popcorn prayers," as my friend Janet calls them, continued throughout the day. The point is not to simply make a list but to ignite a prayer process. Again, it makes me think of Paul's call to "pray without ceasing."

Below are the steps I followed, just to get you thinking about your list:

Your Personal World of Concerns

- I started with my immediate family, David and our children, then our parents and siblings. Though I pray for our family daily, the list guarantees there will be one day each week where I can really focus on their special concerns.

- I then included our inner circle of close friends, neighbors, co-workers, teachers, coaches; adding them to the list forced me to think about the people who were truly important in my life.
- I added my heart's desires and dreams and those of my husband and children.
- I put in specific problems, weaknesses, areas of sin, and broken places in my life or in the lives of those I love.
- Areas I call the "waiting room" prayers—special longings of my heart and those of my family, long-standing desires of friends who wanted to be married, couples longing for children.

AIM BEYOND YOUR PERSONAL CIRCLE

The personal circle is where most people stop, and it's why prayers tend to become self-centered and unhealthy. As I've said, 9/11 made it clear to me that God wants our prayers to stretch around the world—and you'll notice that following suit, much of this book will return to that concept. My friend Lisa says it this way: we aim our prayers out into the world and work our way back to our own personal needs. She calls it a healthy alignment.

So after I listed the personal concerns on my heart, I began to reflect on needs beyond my own. I began asking God what was on His mind. What were the things that mattered to Him? My list in this area grew over time as different people and places grabbed my heart. My daughter, Bethany, wanted to add a country to her list. She asked God to somehow bring a nation to her attention that needed prayer. One night while watching television, she was deeply moved by an a cappella boys' choir—orphans from war-torn Liberia. She suddenly realized that she could pray for them. Liberia now has a spot on her list. As you go about your daily business, be on the lookout for ways to enlarge your own prayer vision.

When you are listing these wider areas of concern, I encourage you to steer clear of vague generalities like "world hunger." Who is hungry? Where do they live? Here are some of the broader items I added to my list.

- After 9/11, I became more sensitive to the heavy load our leaders carry. Key government leaders like the mayor of Charlotte, our governor, and our president made my list.
- Heightened concern for our armed forces and those defending our freedom led me to include the military, the FBI, and the CIA. In time, those became more personal as God brought members of these branches of service into my life.
- Nations I had traveled to or that God had put on my heart through a news story, an article, or a personal encounter with a person from a certain country often sparked my commitment to pray for them.
- I noticed special concerns that captured my heart—like the persecuted church, the homeless, at-risk kids, to name a few.
- I watched for people who randomly intersected my life—and for whom I felt a burden to pray. I kept a little white space in my list—room to add new concerns as they appeared.

Making Your List

Now it's time to write your list. Take some time for reflection and ask God to reveal how He wants you to pray. It will be different for each reader. Don't limit yourself. Put anything on your list that's on your heart. Don't worry about a specific order, or even the number of needs at this point. You can streamline the list later. Remember, you are the only one on planet Earth looking at life from your unique vantage point. I sometimes remind myself that I might be the only person in the whole world praying for a certain person at that precise moment!

Let the following categories simply be a guide as you list your items. You can use the space in this chapter to record your list. Or if you keep a journal, you can devote a page to serve as your Master List. It's important to have this Master List handy for easy reference each morning. You will find that you are occasionally adding or deleting items from this Master List.

My family:

_____

_____

_____

My friends, neighbors, co-workers:

_____

_____

_____

My children's teachers, coaches, etc.:

_____

_____

_____

My pastor and church:

_____

_____

_____

My secret hopes and dreams:

_____

_____

_____

Problems and worries:

_____

_____

_____

Areas of weakness or sin where I need victory:

_____

_____

_____

Waiting room prayers:

_____

_____

_____

Government leaders (president, governor, mayor):

_____

_____

_____

Military, FBI, CIA—defenders of our nation:

_____

_____

_____

Nations God has put on my heart:

_____

_____

_____

Random people or needs that God places on my heart:

_____

_____

_____

New concerns:

_____

_____

_____

NUMBER YOUR LIST

Like me, you probably ended up with something like fifty items on your Master List. Again, don't worry about how many items you have at this point. Then follow these steps:

- Looking at your list, repeatedly number the items 1–7 in the order you wrote them down. Number 1s will be Monday, number 2s Tuesday, Number 3s Wednesday, and so on.
- Don't try to put the items into categories. It may seem like a random collection at first, but you may find, as I did, that God ordered this list Himself.
- I found that from seven to ten items a day was realistic. Researchers tell us that the human brain can easily memorize

seven items, but more than that and we run into problems—thus the development of seven-digit telephone numbers. No wonder I have a hard time remembering our youngest son's number. He has a different area code—ten digits to remember!

- If you have too many items, you can group together a couple of related ones. For instance, I put my sister Janice and her daughter Emily Ann on Thursday. I also group David's sister, Carolyn, and her husband, Dan, along with their children on that day.
- Seven to ten items a day translates into a list of fifty to seventy needs. Remember, this is just a guideline, and there is nothing magical about the number.
- I never tried to memorize my list, especially because I seemed to constantly be adding new "items," but over time, I found that people and even places made their way into my permanent memory. This became valuable as a reminder to pray at various moments in my day when I didn't have my list handy. I also found myself "nudged" to pray more and more as the list continued to become part of my thinking.

THE CHUBBY BOOK METHOD

As I mentioned, I found a wonderful little tool that made my list more portable. I discovered that an ordinary wire-bound booklet of 3x5-inch cards was perfect for my list. It can be found in most grocery or office supply stores. Durable and portable, this is my Chubby Book. A fine-point Sharpie is my favorite—doesn't smear or fade. But of course, the writing utensil you use is up to you.

The Chubby Book method is simple. I'll spell out the method just so you can get a sense of its flow.

Before reading my Bible, I jot down the theme of the day—the attribute of God highlighted in the daily format we learned about earlier.

Then, looking at my Master List, I write the items from that day's prayer list in the Chubby Book. Next I add a few PODs (prayers on demand) that I mentioned in Chapter 3.

Then I read and reflect on a passage of Scripture. I like to follow a Bible reading plan, which provides me with a chapter a day. I consider the following when I read: What is God saying? I stop to listen and ponder. I want to hear God's voice, and especially His whispers. What is He saying to me personally? What is God asking me to do? How am I to pray? What am I to give? Where am I to go?

After reading, I consider the practical application of my reading. The message to me that morning doesn't have to be dramatic, but I do hope it will be relevant and true to the words of Scripture. Sometimes I may quietly receive wisdom or insight. When given a new perspective about a person or a problem, I might ask, *Lord, do I take immediate action in the situation or commit it to further prayer?* The need, I learned, is not always the call. Over time, as I followed this process, I became less eager to fix people and their problems, and more eager to entrust them to God in prayer.

Then I ask God to illuminate a special verse or verses just for me—a watchword—and write that verse on the card facing the list in my Chubby Book. We'll talk more about watchwords and themes in the next section. You can even write down some verses to form your own "arsenal" of verses.

During this quiet time with God, I will often go through my list reflecting on each person, place, or problem and pray that Scripture for each item. The process of reading the Bible and praying over that list varies, but I need at least thirty minutes for this to take root. Gradually, I begin to focus on what God's Word says about the situation, rather than the size and scope of the issue. I heard somewhere that we should "glance at the problem and gaze on the promise."

I must tell you something at this point. I have never liked workbooks. As a child, I even resisted coloring books, but I would copy the pictures freehand and create my own designs on drawing paper. I used the coloring book as a pattern to unleash my own creativity.

That's why I hope the Chubby Book format will help you discover what kind of list works for you. The idea is to develop a prayer habit that is sustainable. I have been following different variations of this pattern for nearly ten years. The flexibility and creativity I have discovered with it keeps prayer fresh. In other words, do what works for you.

Just as a guide, however, on the next page, you'll see an example out of my Chubby Book. I've also included a Quick-Start Method for using a Chubby Book in the "Going Deeper" section (page 225). Some of my "techie" friends use various iPhone apps to keep track of their lists. (They, however, must not accidentally drop theirs in a puddle of water while walking, as I recently did.) The point is, again, to do what works for you.

The Chubby Book has revolutionized my prayer list by making it more portable. The Chinese have a saying that when you pray, it's best to have your hands and feet moving. The list, the verses, and my Chubby Book—these go where I go. No longer does prayer have to stay in the closet. Folding clothes, preparing a meal, making one of my many trips across town, commuting to work, waiting for an appointment—all become opportunities to listen to God.

MY CHUBBY BOOK

John 20:31

"But these are written that
you may believe that Jesus
is the Christ, the son of God,
and that by believing you
may have life in His name."

Daily Theme: PRAISE

Jessie

SEEDS Scholars

Dominique

Mideast: Egypt

Soldier Jesse: Afghanistan

Jonathan & family

Women battling infertility

POD's

Kris and Marisa

Mom's healing

JB's calling

Michael's meet

peace: Sudan

ALARM: Emily

FINDING YOUR WATCHWORDS

Let's go back to our earlier discussion in Chapter 2 about the importance of finding watchwords, or words of Scripture that God has placed on your heart.

As noted earlier, I added daily themes to my prayer structure after reading about Mission India's powerful breakthroughs in spiritually challenging regions of India. These themes will give you a wonderful picture of both God's character and His daily work in your life, along with a framework for your spiritual arsenal of watchwords.

I encourage you to find promises from God's Word to enliven the daily themes and make them your own. For example, on Wednesday, the day I reflect on God's "Miracle-Working Power" as my theme, I may jot down a Scripture about this attribute of God.

I will share some of my verses with you. The idea is to be on the lookout for your own watchwords, verses that particularly apply to some of the cares and concerns on your list. You will find space below to record some of your verses.

MONDAYS: PRAY FOR GOD TO PROHIBIT EVIL

This became a good day for me to confess personal sin. Pray for breakthroughs in tough problems, the defeat of evil, or pulling down strongholds. Remind yourself that God is your Protector and the Protector of those you love.

- "Let us throw off everything that hinders and the sin that so easily entangles, and let us run with perseverance the race marked out for us " (Hebrews 12:1).
- "My prayer is not that you take them out of the world, but that you protect them from the evil one" (John 17:15).

- Your own watchwords:

_____

_____

_____

TUESDAYS: PRAY FOR GOD'S PROVISION

Focus on God's character as your Provider. I began to notice the way God supplied just what I needed, ranging from financial resources to those of time and energy. In what ways do you need God to be your Provider today?

- "And God is able to make all grace abound to you, so that in all things at all times, having all that you need, you will abound in every good work" (2 Corinthians 9:8).
- "Behold, I am the Lord, the God of all flesh. Is there anything too hard for me?" (Jeremiah 32:27).
- God's watchwords for today:

_____

_____

_____

WEDNESDAYS: WATCH FOR GOD'S MIRACLE-WORKING POWER

What challenges or even impossible situations do you face where you need God to give you His strength and power?

- "For God has not given us a spirit of fear, but of power and of love and of a sound mind" (2 Timothy 1:7, NKJV).
- "For when I am weak, then I am strong" (2 Corinthians 12:10b).

- God's personal watchwords for you:

_____

_____

_____

THURSDAYS: ASK FOR GOD'S PROBLEM-SOLVING WISDOM

Where are you encountering roadblocks, problems, dilemmas you can't solve?

- "If any of you lacks wisdom, he should ask God who gives generously to all, without finding fault, and it will be given to him. But when he asks, he must believe and not doubt" (James 1:5, 6).
- "I will make you wise and show you where to go. I will guide you and watch over you" (Psalm 32:8, NCV).
- God's personal watchwords for you:

_____

_____

_____

FRIDAYS: REFLECT ON GOD'S PRESENCE

Be aware of the presence of Christ in your life. Ask Him to reveal Himself in particular ways that you can understand—learn to abide in Him.

- "The Lord replied (to Moses): 'My Presence will go with you and I will give you rest'" (Exodus 33:14).
- "Come to me all you who are weary and burdened and I will give you rest. . . . Learn from me, for I am gentle and humble

in heart, and you will find rest for your souls. For my yoke is easy and my burden is light" (Matthew 11:28–30).

- God's personal watchwords for you:

_____

_____

_____

SATURDAYS: PRAY FOR GOD'S PURPOSE

What is God's calling on your life and those for whom you are praying?

- "I know you can do all things; no plan of yours can be thwarted" (Job 42:2).
- "For we are God's workmanship, created in Christ Jesus to do good works, which God prepared in advance for us to do" (Ephesians 2:10).
- "And now, O Israel, what does the Lord your God ask of you but to fear the Lord your God, to walk in all his ways, to love him, to serve the Lord your God with all your heart and with all your soul, and to observe the Lord's commands and decrees that I am giving you today for your own good?" (Deuteronomy 10:12–13).
- God's personal watchwords for you:

_____

_____

_____

SUNDAYS: PRAISE GOD FOR HIS GOODNESS

Think about God's blessings and His character. Recalibrate your thinking. Look at life through His lenses.

- "Finally, whatever is true, whatever is noble, whatever is right, whatever is pure, whatever is lovely, whatever is admirable—if anything is excellent or praiseworthy—think about such things" (Philippians 4:8).
- "Every good and perfect gift is from above, coming down from the Father of the heavenly lights, who does not change like the shifting shadows" (James 1:17).
- "And I pray that Christ will be more and more at home in your hearts, living within you as you trust in him. May your roots go down deep into the soil of God's marvelous love, and may you be able to feel and understand, as all God's children should, how long, how wide, how deep, and how high his love really is; and to experience this love for yourselves, though it is so great that you will never see the end of it or fully know or understand it. And so at last you will be filled up with God himself" (Ephesians 3:17–19, NLT).
- God's personal watchwords for you:

_____

_____

_____

GETTING TO KNOW GOD

The Chubby Book approach is an easy way to weave your prayer list, themes, and watchwords into your day. More than anything, I hope this method will give you a practical way to get to know God and the unique facets of His personality.

Remember that the point is not a perfect method or list—please don't be legalistic about it. The point is to keep your focus on God's eternal perspective. As you do this, you'll find your prayers gaining substance. They will become more specific, because you will begin to see God's power. He is quite capable of giving real answers to real needs.

Your need simply becomes an opportunity to focus on His power. Your worry can be a reminder to channel that energy into alertness. Your problem has now become an opportunity to lean on His wisdom.

As we add more and more precision to our prayer lives, we learn to watch for God, to listen for His whispers and roars—to become familiar with His character, personality, and love; in other words, you are learning to *abide*. This abiding, Jesus revealed to His followers, is the secret to answered prayer. "If you abide in Me, and My words abide in you, ask whatever you wish, and it will be done for you" (John 15:7, NASB).

I challenge you to put your whole heart into getting to know God, His personality, His will. See Him at work. Ask Him to teach you to see yourself, others, and the world through His eyes. Who is on His heart? How should you pray? What can you give? Where should you go? If you ask Him these questions, you may be surprised at the adventures that follow.

God made each of us different. What works for me might not work for you. I expect you will find a variety of techniques that make the list come alive for you. One friend who began keeping a list found that it also helps her to have a bulletin board in her laundry room where she places pictures of those for whom she prays and notes answers to prayer. My daughter, Bethany, and her husband, Ryan, write prayer requests on rocks and put them in a glass vase on one end of their mantel. When answers come, they sign and date the rock with a Sharpie and put it in the vase on the other side of the mantel, always reminding them of God's continual care for them.

My confidence in prayer grew over time. So did my trust in God.

He didn't change, nor did He love me any more or less because of my commitment to pray, but as I gave my whole heart to try to hear His voice and learn how to pray, the rewards came.

"Devote yourselves to prayer, being watchful and thankful," Paul reminded the Colossians. I was beginning to understand this, too. As my devotion to prayer grew, I became more watchful, I saw more answers, and thankfulness would often rise up in my heart. The list gave me some tangible footholds, making my prayers more precise in nature, but also sustainable over time.

I've heard that it takes twenty-one days to begin to form a new habit. That's what the next chapter is all about: a 21-Day Experiment in taking the next step in seeking God with your whole heart. Approach this with a sense of expectancy, and with hope. Remember, He has promised to reward those "who diligently seek Him."

PART THREE

Pray with Authority

Chapter 5

The 21-Day Experiment

Faith comes from hearing . . . the Word of Christ.

—ROMANS 10:17

My friend Linda loves God's Word more than anyone I know. Linda's husband, Rick Hendrick, happens to be the owner of NASCAR here in the Carolinas. Several years ago, Rick and Linda lost ten family members and friends, including their son, in a highly publicized and devastating private plane crash. "I had nothing—no strength to go on and absolutely nothing to give God," she told me. "He carried me through my time of pain and suffering with His Word. If I could tear out the pages of my Bible and eat them, I would," she says with a smile. Linda now takes that same message of hope each week to female inmates at a maximum-security detention center in a neighboring community. She has learned firsthand about the life-giving power of God's Word. No wonder Linda is so accustomed to hearing the voice of God. She clearly understands the link between God's Word and His voice.

If you want my quick answer on how best to hear the voice of God, I will simply echo Linda by saying, "Read His words." God spent 1,469 pages (in my particular version of the Bible) letting us know much about His personality, His power, His plan, His pattern for living, and, best of all, His promises. God has given us authority through His Word that we appropriate through prayer. It's important that we grasp that amazing concept. One way I've learned to incorporate the power of God's Word into my prayer life is through what I call the 21-Day Experiment.

The 21-Day Experiment, put simply, is a way to discover how God's Word can add power to your prayers—and your life. You've given some attention to becoming alert and watchful. I hope your list is working and that you are becoming comfortable with the daily themes. At this point in my journey, I realized that I was missing something. I needed a practical way to add my daily Bible reading into the mix. For some of you, a regular Bible study time is already a habit. Regardless, this experiment will still be valuable to you as you ask God to speak to you through focused reading and meditation on John's Gospel each day.

Remain in His Word

Before beginning your 21-Day Experiment, I encourage you to pause a minute and reflect on Jesus' words to His disciples in John 15:7: "If you remain in me and my words remain in you, ask whatever you wish and it will be given you." While this clearly doesn't mean that we get everything we want when we want it, the fact remains. There is a powerful link between God's Word and answered prayer. You'll have a chance during the next twenty-one days to combine a reading of God's Word with your Chubby Book method of prayer.

The next twenty-one days could be life changing for you. This experiment will also help you to ask yourself what you believe about Jesus Christ. Who is He to you? I'm glad you're reading this book and I challenge you to stick with the entire twenty-one days, no matter what distractions come your way.

I've shared with you many of the reasons I am committed to learning from God's Word. Simply put, I want to learn to hear God and become familiar with His voice. There is a tremendous link between the authority we have been given through God's Word and our effectiveness in prayer. Remember the second part of our Lord's Prayer, "Your kingdom come, Your will be done on earth as in heaven." And God's will, as we have been learning, is best reflected in His Word. It should stun us into faithfulness to realize that our prayers are part of the way God gets His work done here on earth.

I also want to train myself to hear God's voice through an understanding of His Word because, as I have discovered, there is another voice. When nineteenth-century scholar R. A. Torrey, author of one of my favorite books on prayer, *How to Pray*, was asked why we should learn how to pray, he said simply this: "There is a devil."[1] This other voice has access to our minds as the father of lies. The definition for the word *Satan* is "accuser." The word *devil,* or *diabalos,* means "divider." It's safe to say that the enemy does not want us to hear and do the will of God. So he will attempt to convince us that his voice is the voice of truth, and to that end, he may even sound religious or appear as an "angel of light." But remember, the Bible warns us that his goal is to "kill, steal, and destroy." I want to remain in God's Word so I can follow His instructions, gain His insight into problems, be protected from unseen snares, and be delivered from the devil's messes. The Bible teaches me that I will face daily battles of faith. Bottom line? Hearing God's voice and praying in agreement with His will can help me emerge from the daily fray victorious. And I hope that my prayers might help those I love in their battles, too.

YOUR PERSONAL EXPERIMENT

When I was a new believer, I came across a book that had a great impact on my understanding of the power of God's Word. Former atheist and newspaper reporter Emily Gardiner Neal captivated me with her story. Just a year earlier, I, too, had been an atheistic journalism major in college. *The Healing Power of Christ* tells of her personal transformation after reading the Gospel of John, not as a believer, but as a skeptic.[2] Instead of confirming her assertion that the Bible was a dead book, her "laboratory experiment" opened her eyes to the reality of Christ. Neal began to challenge others to set aside twenty-one days to read John, just one chapter a day. I periodically use this simple spiritual exercise to revive my faith.

Each time I perform my own 21-Day Experiment, God speaks in a tangible way. It occurs more often as a whisper than a shout, but it is always personal, just for me. I will show you how to incorporate the Chubby Book method into this simple Bible reading plan.

GROUND RULES

- Make a decision to stick with this 21-Day Experiment. Do not evaluate whether it works or if any changes occur until the end of the twenty-one days. You may even say to yourself, *Well, nothing seems to be happening today, but I will postpone judging its impact until after twenty-one days.*
- The main purpose of the experiment is for Jesus to become more real to you and for God's Word to come alive. Answered prayer is a by-product.

THE DAILY PATTERN

- Set aside fifteen minutes each day to prayerfully read one chapter of John's Gospel. Remember, there are twenty-one chapters. Pray for God to impress a verse or two upon your mind for that day. Write that watchword in your Chubby Book.

- On the adjacent card, list your seven to ten cares for that day of the week. (Refer back to your Master List in Chapter 4.)
- Inspired by what you read from John, pray for each of the needs you listed. Sometimes I will pray the verse from John in the form of a promise for that person. Other times I will pray through The Lord's Prayer for them.
- It takes just about a minute for each care. As I mentioned before, I often pray over this list again as I go for a walk, do dishes, wait in the carpool line. Sometimes I will meditate on or even memorize the verse from John.
- I pray for God to help me notice subtle answers throughout the day. Psalm 5:3 says, "In the morning, O LORD, You will hear my voice; in the morning, I will order *my prayer* to You and *eagerly* watch" (NASB).

PERSONAL REFLECTION

As I continued to practice my daily habit of reading God's Word and prayer, I noticed a number of changes. I've mentioned that I worried less—especially since it was becoming a reflex to channel my worries into prayers. By bringing my fears, weaknesses, sins, problems, worries, dreams, hopes, and heart's desires straight to my encounters with God, I gave Him first shot at filling those needs. While reading the Bible, I could expect a particular verse or passage to warm my heart—these verses became my own arsenal of watchwords. Sometimes the words seemed to leap off the page and into my heart, putting anxiety to flight. I continued the practice of "glancing at the problem and gazing on the promise," as a friend often said. My heart was at rest even before I got to see answers to prayer with my eyes.

I also seemed to have fewer bursts of temper. After all, when I didn't see it as my job to play God and try to fix everybody, I was less likely to get angry when they didn't change according to my plans. And with all the energy I didn't spend on worry and anger, I seemed to have more energy for the work God *had* called me to do, whether at home with my family, leading Bible studies, or being available for His work in the world.

As a by-product of this energy, I was also becoming more "self-controlled and alert," reflecting the truth of the Bible verse (1 Peter 4:7) that grabbed my attention in my car on 9/11: "The end of all things is near. Therefore be alert and self-controlled so you can pray." I had to believe this was making a difference in my prayers.

At the end of your twenty-one days, I encourage you to spend some time alone, reflecting on what you have observed. Please don't rush through this part of the exercise. It's worth the time to get quiet and unplug from all the mind-numbing noise around you to ponder what God may have been saying to you.

I find it helps to journal as I ask myself some questions: Have I noticed God at work in my life during these twenty-one days? Am I more in tune with His voice? If this is your first experience reading the Bible, what is your opinion of Jesus?

Sometimes, it helps to have a friend do this experiment with you. The accountability is good. At the end of twenty-one days, compare your experiences. You may discover, like I did, that having a prayer partner to agree with you in prayer on a regular basis is powerful and the shared experiences of the 21-Day Experiment add richness to your journey. (More on prayer partners in Chapter 7, "Teammates.")

Thanks to technology, God's Word has never been easier to read throughout the day. There are a variety of applications that allow you to download the entire Bible onto your mobile devices—many of them are free.[3] Some are interactive, allowing you to tweet or share comments with others. Be creative about when and where to read your Bible, during and after the experiment. One woman I know even used her iPhone to meditate on God's Word while stuck in a line at Walmart.

Pennies from Heaven

I use this 21-Day Experiment whenever my faith needs a pick-me-up. And while my faith has been refreshed each time I've tried this approach, one instance will always stand out in my mind—that particular time I felt God truly whispered His love for me.

David and I were ten years into our work at Forest Hill Church in Charlotte. Fresh-faced and eager, we had plunged into our ministry with big dreams. The congregation had outgrown its small building and numbered around 1,500 members. We had relocated the church, built a home, and had two of our children in the previous three years. Our zeal remained fervent, but the pace was breathtaking at times.

Prayer had become my lifeline and I had lots to pray about. I don't remember the first penny that caught my eye, but for months I had been noticing pennies in the strangest places. Sometimes I would discover one at my feet, just after I had prayed. *Funny*, I thought, *it's almost as though God wants to let me know that He hears my prayers. Could these pennies really be little messages of encouragement from God?* Perhaps it was just coincidence or wishful thinking, argued my rational mind. After all, the world groans with the weight of major crises. God has better things to do than send me pennies.

Still I hoped, and there it was. Another penny—this one in the heel of my shoe. The last one had been under a glass in the kitchen, and the one before that, right in the middle of my bed!

I began saving these "pennies from heaven" in a pretty jar in my kitchen. Sometimes I would drop in a little note about where I found the penny and date it as a memory. Over the next months the pennies continued to appear. And my jar continued to fill.

That spring I attended a weekend prayer retreat. My hunger for God peaked as I experienced powerful prayer with women of all ages. I shared my "penny story" with Kenna, a friend who was on the retreat. I knew she understood, for her relationship with the Lord was strong. Somehow I felt God drawing me into a deeper understanding of who He was.

I came back from the retreat renewed. I was reminded of the first 21-Day Experiment that I had originally performed as a new believer, and I decided that it was time to try it again. I began reading a chapter of John a day, meditating on a special verse that seemed to hold particular meaning for me.

When I got to day twenty, I was deeply touched by the man we know as Doubting Thomas (John 20:24–29). Thomas had not been present when Jesus appeared to the other disciples after His resurrection. I don't know why Thomas missed the first showing, but I could imagine how his face fell as the disciples excitedly told him, "We have seen the Lord!"

With words that I think must have dripped with discouragement, he vowed, "Unless I see the nail marks in his hands and put my finger where the nails were . . . I will not believe." Still, Thomas continued to hang around the disciples, maybe hoping that Jesus had not forgotten him.

I felt for Thomas. I, too, had sometimes struggled with doubt.

But when Jesus appeared again eight days later, He singled out Thomas, and instead of scolding him for his wavering faith, Jesus spoke directly to Thomas's deepest longing for concrete proof of the resurrected Christ. "Put your finger here," He told Thomas. "See my hands," He said. "Reach out your hand and put it into my side," He added. "Stop doubting and believe." Thomas gasped, I am sure, as he cried out, "My Lord and my God."

Something about those verses arrested me, and I reflected. Could it be that God is really the kind of God who encourages sincere doubters like Thomas and, sometimes, like me? If true, then He would surely send pennies of encouragement to an honest seeker, I reasoned. *Lord,* I prayed silently, *I do believe You are sending those pennies as a way of strengthening my faith.* Almost as an afterthought, I added these words: *And Lord, You did it for Thomas. Somehow, I want to see Your nail marks, too.* I never told anyone about that prayer because I didn't expect God to answer such an impossible request.

A few days later, I received a card in the mail from Kenna. "Dear Marilynn," she wrote, "I found this penny in my dryer and I thought of you. Perhaps the Lord sent this penny as an encouragement to us both."

Suddenly, I caught my breath. Taped to her card was the penny. But as I looked closer, I saw something that held me in awe. It was just an ordinary penny. But right through its center was a nail hole. I sat transfixed. And I knew. God had sent me my own nail mark, just as I'd prayed. And for a moment, I felt a bit like Thomas, touching the nail hole in Jesus' hand.

Then and there, I decided. My God is awesome and powerful enough to rule the world. He is also personal and tender enough to send a nail-pierced penny to another Doubting Thomas like me, in need of encouragement.

I shared this story years later with a gathering of women on a retreat. One woman was inspired to use the penny idea as a way to raise money for a retreat center for missionaries working with women in Muslim countries. She called the project "Pennies for a Haven."

Why not embark on your 21-Day Experiment and see what happens! And I hope you share your experience with me. I've set up a blog (http://marilynnchadwick.com) to be a community of voices of those who've gone through this journey.

It's amazing. It doesn't matter how many times I do the 21-Day Experiment; God always seems to find a fresh way to communicate His love for me. I imagine He wants to reinforce my habit of prayer and Bible reading as much as I want to stick with it. I keep reminding myself, I want to run the race strong.

Chapter 6

Growing Deeper

*One day Jesus was praying in a certain place. When he finished, one of
his disciples said to him, "Lord, teach us to pray . . ."*

—Luke 11:1

Years ago, when playing basketball for the University of North
Carolina, my husband asked his coach, the legendary Dean Smith,
how he could help make the Tar Heels a stronger team. As David
tells the story, Smith simply said, "David, you can help the team
most if you become a better player."[1] I love that advice when it comes
to prayer. If I want to make a difference in the world, it makes sense
that I become a better "pray-er."

After all, since I had discovered a heart to pray for the world,
I was often on the lookout for trade secrets. As I've said before, I
wanted my prayers to work. I wanted to access the power available
in prayer through God's Word, and I was continuing to grasp the
importance of biblical authority in shaping an effective prayer life.

Maybe, as you've gone along this prayer journey with me, you've
begun to feel like I did as you discover some of the power available
through God's Word. When I read about some of the most important

pray-ers in Scripture, I realized I had only scratched the surface when it came to hearing His voice. I was hungry to go deeper.

Growing Deeper

I've talked a lot about some of the places this prayer journey took me—even as far away as Africa. I've also shared its impact on my own spiritual growth. It's not healthy to become too absorbed with looking at our own benchmarks. But I must admit, it was really encouraging to experience a growing freedom in areas that had troubled me, such as worry and anger.

That's why I want to encourage you to stay faithful and persevere as you develop your habits of staying alert, reading God's Word, watching, and listening. Even when prayer seemed hard, I would rather have slept, or I wondered if anything was happening, I kept on praying. I trusted that if I remained faithful to this process, then my prayers would have a tangible impact on the world outside my little world.

I have found a couple in-depth resources to be incredibly helpful in my prayer journey. We've already discussed the Mueller method—letting prayer flow from a meditative reading of Scripture—and the daily themes, which inspire us to shape our prayers with a focus on one unique attribute of God. We have our Master Lists and our Chubby Books, which, as I hope you have already found, are wonderful ways to forge a more precise prayer life. But what I'd like to share with you now are resources that will help you grow deeper in your understanding of scripturally based prayer.

RESOURCE 1: MY BIG FAT GREEK BIBLE

A surprising discovery, which opened the door to a better understanding of praying with biblical authority, came in the form of a Greek Study Bible. This useful resource gave me more keys to unlocking Scripture. My "Big Fat Greek Bible," as I like to call it, may look formidable next to the simple little Chubby Book. And actually, it's the single most important Bible study tool I've ever found. Ever. Its proper name is the *Hebrew-Greek Key Word Study Bible*.[2] My Big Fat Greek Bible is leather, so it stands up to a lot of wear and tear. You can purchase this sturdy volume for the cost of a pair of running shoes—on sale.

This unique Bible has a couple of special features, including a concordance and Greek-Hebrew dictionary. The concordance in the back, a time-tested Bible study aid, enabled me to find all the places where a particular word was used. A concordance is a must-have if you want a better grasp of Scripture. The Hebrew and Greek Language Aids, also in the back of my Greek Bible, provide information normally found only in the lexicons and commentaries.

I know this information may sound daunting, but the editor of this particular *Key Word Study Bible* has done the hard work in advance. The significant, or "key," words are simply numbered, so if you can count, you can use this fabulous tool. You find a word that has meaning for you and flip to the corresponding number in the back to find its expanded definition in the original Hebrew or Greek writing.

This Greek Study Bible helped me link prayer to the many promises in God's Word. Even my friends who don't typically enjoy words as much as I do have agreed that this is a wonderful addition to the Chubby Book method. These studies can really contribute to the way you approach your watch words, your attributes, and your list.

Here's an example. By searching the concordance for *fear*, I was able to add power and precision to my prayers to overcome this troublesome enemy. First, I learned all the places where fear is mentioned in the Bible. I drew strength from Paul's challenge to young Timothy to stand against the ugly foe of fear. He encourages Timothy (and us) by reminding him, "For God has not given us a spirit of fear, but of power and of love and of a sound mind" (2 Timothy 1:7, NKJ).

Next, in looking at the corresponding number for *sound mind,* I discovered that the Greek word *sophronismos,* as shown in the accompanying dictionary, can also be translated as "self-discipline." It's derived from the very same word for "self-controlled" in the 1 Peter 4:7 verse that had been my anchor since 9/11: "Be self-controlled and alert so you can pray."

Again, the lesson was reinforced. God does not give fear. To the contrary, His spirit provides power, love, and a sound mind. Not only relevant to our mental health, this promise links the importance of self-control to the process of and power in prayer. Now I understood why the list and Chubby Book—which were bringing more discipline to my prayer life—were also weapons in the battle against fear. Over and over, I seemed to be learning the same lesson: prayer is best when it's birthed out of human need and grounded in God's Word.

RESOURCE 2: JESUS' RECIPE FOR WORLD-CHANGING PRAYER

Jesus' disciples must have been in constant awe of His work. After all, they had seen Him heal the sick, raise the dead, and drive out demons. But it's incredible to realize that they never asked Him to teach them how to perform miracles. They only asked Him how to pray. "Lord, teach us to pray," they said (Luke 11:1).

Remember that many of Jesus' followers were rough-and-tumble fishermen. Their work was exhausting and dangerous. Life had toughened these men. So, a shrewd teacher, Jesus first taught them how not to pray. When you pray, don't be like the hypocrites who pray in public to be seen by others. "Instead," He told them, "go into your room, close the door and pray to your Father." The Father "sees what is done in secret," Jesus assured them. He "will reward you." And by the way, don't keep on babbling like those who pray long-winded prayers. He added, "Your Father knows what you need even before you ask Him" (Matthew 6:6–8).

You don't have to pray out loud in public, you don't have to use lots of words, and you are praying to your Father, who already knows what you need. Sounds pretty user-friendly—even to a bunch of fishermen. So where can you pray? Alone with God, of course! Which meant they could pray throughout their day—while they fished, while they cleaned the catch, on the long walk home. They could hear God's voice anywhere.

"This is how you should pray," Jesus told them. He proceeded to give a short, but power-packed tutorial that has come to be known the world over as The Lord's Prayer. It really should be called The Disciple's Prayer. The word for *disciple* simply means "student or learner." If you want to learn what Jesus has to say about prayer, then you, too, are a disciple.

It helps to understand that Jesus' instructions are simply training tips on how to pray. Instead of a rote prayer, The Lord's Prayer is really a recipe for effective prayer. His outline gives you all the ingredients, or fundamentals, of a prayer life that is biblical, balanced, and full of power. Sounds like world-changing prayer, doesn't it? Just what I was looking for!

Though it's possible to pray through the outline of The Lord's Prayer in order, I prefer to look at its ingredients the way I would a balanced diet. I may not always eat my proteins, vegetables, grains, and fruit in a certain order. But I know a well-balanced diet must include all those elements. Such a balance helps me to stay strong and healthy, able to fight off the disease of illness and injury.

In much the same way, The Lord's Prayer, when followed, gives us a well-balanced prayer diet. We are strengthened by the combination of praise, thanksgiving, petition, and confession. We fight off temptation, are delivered from evil, and make ready for action.

In response to His disciples' heartfelt request for help with prayer, Jesus answered with seven short training tips.

"This, then, is how you should pray:

- 'Our Father in heaven, hallowed be your name,
- your kingdom come, your will be done, on earth as it is in heaven.
- Give us today our daily bread.
- And forgive us our debts,
- as we also have forgiven our debtors.
- And lead us not into temptation,
- but deliver us from the evil one' (Matthew 6:9–13, NIV; bullets added).

The Protein of Prayer

Praise: "Our Father in heaven, hallowed be your name."

The Bible actually speaks more about praise than it does prayer. I call it the "protein of prayer." *Protein* comes from a Greek word meaning "of first importance." I am more of a pragmatist than a mystic. I can't tell you why praise lifts my spirits and sometimes turns around situations faster than endless amounts of asking. It just does. Praise is like a one-two punch to the solar plexus of the enemy. Praise prompts breakthroughs in my prayers.

God is magnificent beyond words or understanding. He resides in heaven, but He is also mysteriously present in and with us through His Holy Spirit. It's important to saturate yourself in an understanding of God's character. That's the reason I continue to focus on daily themes and the attributes of His character. When I catch a glimpse of who God really is and what He has done, praise and thanksgiving naturally follow.

Often it helps me to read a portion of Scripture like Psalm 145 and actually underline God's attributes to remind myself of who He is: "great, most worthy of praise, abundant in goodness, righteous, gracious, compassionate, slow to anger, rich in love, good to all, faithful to all His promises, near to all who call on Him, and watching over all who love Him."

Thanksgiving: I look at thanksgiving as "praise in detail." You know by now that I love lists. Sometimes I make a list of my blessings, even if it's just a mental list. This helps me focus on God's work around me. What has happened in just the last twenty-four hours that made my heart sing? What blessings remain constant?

Jesus encourages us to approach God with an awareness that He is holy, powerful, awe-inspiring. Yet, He reminds us that we are praying not to an impersonal master or army general, but to our Father. He even calls God "Abba," which is better translated as "Daddy."

Think about it. We are God's dearly loved children. This is radically different from any other world religions, all of which teach some variation of the theme of how we must follow some set of laws or principles to work our way to God. As my husband often says, there are not thousands of world religions—there are only two. We must either do something to become righteous, or we accept what Jesus has done for us on the cross. Simply put, "It's either *do*—or *done*." And as I've said earlier, no one is perfectly righteous. That's why Christ's death on the cross was necessary to bring us into God's family.

Maybe your view of God has been too small. I know mine often is. Praise and thanksgiving will help you focus on His greatness. Daily, as I enlarge my view of God through praise, my own problems appear smaller.

God's Wish List

Petition: "Your kingdom come, your will be done, on earth as it is in heaven."

Jesus does something counterintuitive here. He encourages us to pray for the world with as much passion as we do for our own needs. Pressing needs may often compel us to go to God for immediate help before we can even think about needs beyond our own nose. The point is that prayer for the needs of the world is of primary importance in our prayer life. Jesus instructs us to pray for God's will to be done on earth, like it is in heaven. In heaven, God's will is done perfectly—so heaven should be the template for our earthly prayers. The word *thelema* means "will, desire, inclination, or choice." It also means a "want or desire which creates joy—a wish." Think about it. God is asking us to pray for His wishes to come true on earth!

It's significant that Jesus is challenging us to speak with His authority in our prayers for the larger world as well as for our personal needs. This petition is actually (in the Greek) an imperative—more of a demand than a request. It is better translated as "Kingdom come! Will be done on earth!" I often think maybe Jesus wants us to stamp our feet, shake our fists, and shout a bit as we speak God's

Word for His will to be done on a fallen earth that is still crawling with enemies. Such victories in battle don't come without a fight, or without God's Word as our authority. The Bible calls this the fight of faith, and reminds us it's a "good fight" (1 Timothy 1:18). It's clear Jesus wants us to have a global perspective to our prayers, and a heavenly perspective about our results.

It must be said here that I not only pray with Christ's authority, I need to be under His authority for this relationship to work. That sounds so confining—to be under authority. But I liken it to a fortress of power and protection rather than a prison. Yes, I do submit to and obey God's Word, His expressed authority. But this is a good thing, a creative thing, a powerful thing. And where it seems to draw a boundary on my behavior, I know it's for my good because I have grown to trust the character of this wonderful Father.

I remind myself daily that I am praying with authority when I claim God's Word and pray it into the situations I see all around me. Peter even said that God gave us His "very great and precious promises so that through them you may participate in the divine nature, and escape the corruption in the world . . ." (2 Peter 1:4).

Our Wish Lists

Petition for Daily Needs: "Give us today our daily bread."

The Lord knows we have needs. "Don't worry," Jesus says. He even reminded His disciples that unlike unbelievers who "run after" the basic necessities of life, they had a heavenly Father who "knows what you need." "Seek first his kingdom and his righteousness and all these other things would be given to you as well" (Matthew 6:33).

God has designed prayer to be strategic enough to impact nations and nimble enough to address our personal worries. The word in this verse for *daily bread* is used only once in the entire New Testament. Early Bible translators had a tough time finding its meaning until the discovery of an ancient papyrus that turned out to be, of all things, a kind of shopping list. And daily bread means just that—a family's bread just for that day.

Jesus is reminding us to go to God, list in hand, for the most basic needs of daily life. What do you need? What do others need? We are encouraged to ask. Scripture tells us, "Don't worry about anything; instead, pray about everything. Tell God what you need" (Philippians 4:6, NLT).

Real needs, real bread, and a real God who is a Rewarder by His very nature. He wants us to come to Him with confidence when we ask Him to meet our needs. He prefers we go to Him rather than to a less reputable source. Our dreams, our wants, even our wishes. As long as these align with God's Word, we may take those heart's desires to God. A line in an old hymn captures the essence of God's character as a loving father who gives good gifts to His children: "Sweet hour of prayer, sweet hour of prayer, that calls me from a world of care. And bids me at my Father's throne make all my wants and wishes known!"[3]

The most important daily bread is not the physical bread, but the spiritual food of God's Word. Man doesn't only live by bread, Jesus told His listeners, but by "every Word from the mouth of God."

Yes, The Lord's Prayer encourages us to align ourselves with God's larger purposes on earth, seeking His kingdom impact as a top priority. But we are also on solid footing when we pray for our own needs. As we go to Him on a regular basis, watchful for answers and remembering to be thankful, our trust in God naturally grows stronger. So how specific should we be in asking for "daily bread"? Specific enough so we recognize the answer when it comes!

Admit it, Quit it, Forget it!
Confession: "And forgive us our debts . . ."

I found that prayer could be blocked by my sin, which circularly would be illuminated by my prayer. What if I had lost my temper with David or the children? It was hard to pray. Maybe I was harboring bitterness toward someone. Perhaps I had slipped back into old fear patterns and was trying to control everyone and everything around me. When that happened, I found prayer to be more difficult than usual. Jesus knew that as we grow closer to God, we often come face-to-face with our shortcomings. Raw honesty with God about my sins and weaknesses can be painful, though ultimately freeing.

Confession, also a form of prayer, allows us to bring the daily struggles to Him for forgiveness and cleansing. God knows how important confession and forgiveness are to both our prayer life and our spiritual health. "Confess your sins to each other and pray for each other so that you may be healed," His Word promises (James 5:16). Confession is an area where a prayer partner can be a big help. Hebrews 3:13 tells us to encourage each other daily "so that none of you will be hardened by sin's deceitfulness." I'll talk more about the importance of a prayer partner in the next chapter. Sometimes we would call each other with a quick admission of our struggles. "I'm struggling with worry today. I'm going to replace that fear with faith." Or, "I need to keep my big mouth quiet—pray I will have strength!"

I've heard that the founder of Campus Crusade for Christ International, Bill Bright, and his wife, Vonette, took confession seriously. They would even read through the Ten Commandments at the end of each day and admit areas of sin and struggle. It's been said that we don't break the Ten Commandments—they break us.

The law is a road map, but its most important purpose is to point to our need for Jesus.

As I became more practiced in prayer, I caught myself in problem areas before they became a big deal. I went to God earlier about my faulty thinking and behavior. More and more, the Holy Spirit often gently nudged me toward confession and repentance. As someone wisely said, "It's best to keep short accounts with God." Another of Coach Smith's coaching tips in basketball applies to repentance. When you make a mistake in basketball, as in life, it helps to "admit it, quit it, and forget it!"

As We Forgive

Confession: ". . . as we also have forgiven our debtors."

When teaching us about roadblocks to effective prayer, Jesus goes straight to one culprit, which causes everything from resentment to world wars: unforgiveness. "Forgive us our sins, as we also forgive those who sin against us." In a single petition, He sweeps out guilt and bitterness, and everything in between. I couldn't escape the fact that my experience of God's forgiveness was inseparably linked to my forgiveness of those who had wounded me.

Sometimes prayer feels a little like death. That is especially true in this area of laying down my rights and forgiving someone. Ruthless honesty is crucial here. John tells us if we say we are without sin, we are deceiving ourselves. Forgiveness is available simply for the asking. If we confess our sins, He is faithful to forgive us and clean up our act (1 John 1:8, 9). If it seems too easy, remember that this forgiveness cost God everything in the death of Jesus. His expectation is that we extend that grace to other human beings, who are just as flawed as we are. And just in case we didn't get it the first time, Jesus follows His instruction on The Lord's Prayer with a final reminder about forgiveness (Matthew 6:14, 15). If you don't forgive others, your Heavenly Father will not forgive you. Got it?

Lead Us Gently

Guidance: "And lead us not into temptation . . ."

I'm amazed at the number of times Jesus said, "Watch out!" He warns us the way any good parent would. Watch out for greed, look out for hypocrisy, avoid idolatry, watch and pray so you don't fall into temptation, watch out for false teachers, watch for my return!

Knowing we need wisdom to avoid the snares set by the evil one, Jesus reminds us to be alert and pray for discernment. Some people seem to pray for miracle after miracle—personally, I'd like to learn a little more "preventive prayer." I am willing to take the time to go slowly, listen for God's guidance, watch for His leading, and find wisdom in a multitude of counselors.

My young friend Isaiah, an outstanding college campus leader, just completed his senior year at Morehouse College in Atlanta. His father, a single parent raising seven children in a fragile community, made it a habit to have the children read a chapter a day from the book of Proverbs. The first two boys achieved scholarships at Davidson College, near Charlotte. The next sister in line after Isaiah went to Dartmouth. They have learned to follow God's plan for their lives and avoid the temptations rampant in their neighborhood. This wise father found practical ways to help his children avoid pitfalls. Surely our Heavenly Father will do likewise for His children—if we will listen.

Rescue 911

Deliverance: ". . . but deliver us from the evil one."

The devil prowls like a lion seeking someone to devour. We are encouraged to remain alert to his schemes (1 Peter 5:8). I prefer to pray for God to lead me away from temptation. That's Plan A. But if we stumble into sin, as humans are famous for doing, Jesus gives us our next line of defense, or Plan B, adding that we are to pray, "deliver us from the evil one." There are times when we simply can't avoid falling into a trap. That's when we cry out to God for help. The Greek word for *deliver*, *rhyomai*, literally means to "snatch from danger, or rescue." I think this must be the spiritual equivalent of a 911 call!

The Bible is full of examples of God's delivering us from actual physical danger, disease, and catastrophe. But we must remember we are occupants of a fallen planet. Thus, our battles are primarily spiritual ones. In the Bible, deliverance has a larger, eternal meaning and indicates the salvation from guilt and the punishment of sin.

The Old Testament Hebrew word *yesuah* means "deliverance, salvation, or victory." The very name of Jesus comes from this root and means "savior." We may be no match for the devil, but Jesus was the overwhelming conqueror through His cross and resurrection (Colossians 2:14, 15). It's in His strength and with His armor that we do battle. Jesus spent His time on earth delivering people from the power of darkness. No wonder the crowds cried out "Hosanna!" as He made His triumphal entry (Matthew 21:9). This exclamation of praise is also traceable to the word *yesuah*. In a very real sense, Jesus Himself is the answer to our prayers for deliverance!

Mad Fan

The declarations and petitions in The Lord's Prayer are comprehensive. Believe me, you could spend hours in prayer using the format. As I've described, it also provides a good framework or recipe to ensure that your prayer life is balanced. Above all, this tutorial from the Master Himself sets you on solid ground to pray with power and with the authority of God's Word.

Yet, I have found that I don't need to commit hours a day to Jesus' format to see results. I can pause and pray for someone on my list, mentally walking through the outline, asking God's work on his or her behalf in about one minute—without rushing! I began setting my cell phone alarm to go off at noon every day to remind me to be a "Mad Fan" for special people on my list. I pray "A Minute a Day for a Need" right at noon. Maybe you will pick a nation, as I did with the Sudan, and pray a minute a day for a nation. Many of my friends have also become a "mad fan." Occasionally, I hear a cell phone alarm going off in a restaurant at noon—and I wonder, *Is someone praying?*

I didn't realize it at the time but during World War II an adviser to Prime Minister Winston Churchill organized a group of people who dropped what they were doing every day at a prescribed hour for one minute to collectively pray for the safety of England, its people, and peace.

And now a group of people are organizing to do the same thing in America. If you would like to participate, take one minute every evening (at 9:00 p.m. Eastern, 8:00 p.m. Central, 7:00 p.m. Mountain, and 6:00 p.m. Pacific), stop whatever you are doing, and spend one minute praying for the safety of the United States, our leaders, our troops, our citizens, and for a return to a godly nation.

RESOURCE 3: PERSEVERANCE

I was amused to hear a friend of mine describe her small daughter's plaintive cry at not getting her way: "But, Mom, all I want is what I *want* when I want it." We live in a world that loves quick answers to tough problems. I've talked a lot about results in prayer. But I don't want you to forget that prayer often requires perseverance, especially when we are walking through tough times. James encourages us to look at trials as a testing of our faith and a chance to develop perseverance. "Perseverance," he reminds us, "must finish its work so that you may be mature and complete, not lacking anything . . ." (James 1:3, 4). I'll talk more about perseverance, or what I like to call "wait training," in Chapter 9.

Perhaps you are wondering how long I prayed for the world before I saw any results. My prayers required the "resource" of perseverance well after the initial crisis of 9/11 settled down.

I've shared with you the story of Zaki, or "Sudan Sam," and our chance encounter during our mission to deliver the Sacks of Hope.[4] But remember that I started praying for the nation of the Sudan just after 9/11 in 2001. My feet didn't actually touch Sudanese soil until the trip in spring of 2008.

That means I prayed for the Sudan for nearly seven years before I saw answers with my own eyes. During those years of praying for the Sudan, I didn't pray volumes, just about a minute on Mondays. I was continually alert to any mention of the Sudan in the news. I am sure, to use my friend Janet's term, I prayed lots of "popcorn" prayers over the years. I was mindful to follow Paul's prayer tip in 1 Timothy 2:1 to "pray for kings and all those in authority, so we could have peaceful lives." I asked God to help me persevere in prayer. *Lord, please don't let me forget the people of the Sudan,* I'd sometimes pray.

Occasionally I was reminded to say a quick prayer for the president of South Sudan, whoever he was. Knowing that Osama bin Laden had a training camp in that region, I also prayed for the president's protection and that God would sweep away the evil that had invaded that region. South Sudan was not an official country at that point, but the Comprehensive Peace Agreement in 2005 ended the war and gave them a measure of autonomy. They would have the opportunity to vote for their independence in 2011.

During our spring 2008 visit to the Sudan, David and I traveled with our team, led by our friend Ken Isaacs, vice president of programs and government relations for Samaritan's Purse. Samaritan's Purse and Isaacs had remained a constant and courageous presence, providing relief throughout the civil war as the South fought to free itself from decades of oppression by the North. As a result, Isaacs had won the hearts of key leaders. Friendships formed on the battlefield go deep. During our visit, Isaacs arranged for us to meet with the president of South Sudan, a war hero instrumental in the South's fight for freedom. His Excellency Salva Kiir welcomed us warmly into his office in Juba, the capital of the South.

Imagine my delight as we met with Salva Kiir for over an hour, hearing about his love for his people and his plans to rebuild their country. Anything we could do to strengthen the local church would best serve his nation, Kiir told us. Pastors and the local churches had been key figures in the nation's brave struggle for freedom.

I glanced around at his office, still amazed at where this journey had taken me. Suddenly my eyes landed on a beach ball globe perched on a table near where I was sitting. A beach ball globe in the office of a national leader? Our children had one just like it at home. And again, globes were one of my prayer triggers to remind me to pray for the world. I just had to laugh—inwardly of course.

I had remembered to take the Prayer Journal that I began soon after 9/11—the one that had recorded my early prayers for the Sudan. By now it was tattered and worn. After our conversation, I waited behind to see Salva Kiir and quietly said to him, "Your Excellency, I wanted to show you this entry in my journal dated

October 11, 2001." He paused as I opened the page and showed him the faded journal entry. "That's when I began praying for you and for South Sudan. I just wanted you to know that God has not forgotten you. He reminded me—just an ordinary mother halfway around the world—to pray for you. And, sir, I promise to keep praying." He shook my hand and we departed. I caught my breath as I walked away from that encounter. A man, a head of state, was no longer just a name on my list—I had listened as he described the things on his heart, I had shaken his hand, I had looked into his eyes. How could this be happening?

Next on our agenda was a visit to the headquarters of Major General Thomas Cirillo, commander of the South Sudanese army during the war. Cirillo greeted Ken Isaacs like a comrade. And no wonder. Isaacs had risked his own life, driving a jeep onto the battlefield to rescue Cirillo's wounded soldiers.

I glanced around our meeting room, which was round with a thatched roof in typical African fashion. But it was air-conditioned and had comfortable furnishings—giving it an East-meets-West feeling. The kind general graciously spent more than an hour telling us about his fight for freedom from the Islamic extremist regime under which his people had suffered for more than two decades.

Speaking in near-perfect English, he described his hopes for a free nation. A committed Christian, he was earnest in his desire for the people of the Sudan to have freedom. "We will not force them to be Christians. If they are animists or Muslims, they should be free to worship as they please. All we want"—he paused for a minute, searching for the right words—"is liberty and justice for all the people of the Sudan."

I pondered all this man had endured and the price he had paid for freedom. Often shielded from much of the world's brutal suffering, we in America caught a glimpse of the horrible reality of evil on 9/11. The people of the South Sudan and other places faced this kind of terror up close and personal on a daily basis.

I was sobered by the stories of horrific suffering I had heard thus far in our journey. How could I forget the firsthand accounts of Sudanese pastors who had witnessed rapes, murders, burnings of their churches, and torture—even of children? All for their faith. Yet the pastors and churches had grown stronger during this time. And as Christians throughout the centuries have survived times of persecution, the communities of faith in South Sudan were vibrant and committed to rebuilding their nation.

Cirillo continued, "This compound where we are meeting was actually used by Osama bin Laden as his training camp during the war." Then Cirillo glanced my way and said to me, "And bin Laden had this room as his meeting place. He probably sat right where you are sitting now."

No one in the room knew the significance of that comment. But I knew. I sat transfixed. I thought back to that newspaper article in October of 2001, telling of bin Laden's location in South Sudan—which nudged me to pray for what seemed at the time to be a remote and somewhat frightening nation. Now I was sitting in the place that had been the target of my prayers. Prayer for the Sudan had come full circle.

During a subsequent visit to the United States the next winter, Salva Kiir stopped at the office of Samaritan's Purse in Boone, North Carolina. David and I were graciously invited to the small gathering. Kiir greeted us warmly with a hug. I sat around the table with a dozen in attendance to hear his words of thanks for the courageous work of Samaritan's Purse in the Sudan.

I was a bit in awe and I wondered. The brave work of many like

Salva Kiir, Thomas Cirillo, and others would have surely gone on without my prayers. But would I have had the privilege of seeing this work of God in the Sudan? Would I have felt such solidarity with the Christians who had suffered and even died for their faith? Men, women, and children who had survived by running into the mountains, living off tree leaves and boiled shoe leather. Would I have been able to look into the eyes of those fellow believers and seen their courage up close and personal had I not prayed? I don't think so. For if I had not been praying for the Sudan and been alert to hear God's voice, I'm not sure I would have been listening when the call came.

God had yet another blessing to add to my ten-year prayer adventure. The people of South Sudan voted in 2011 to become an official nation, the 193rd to be exact. Salva Kiir was elected as president in a 99 percent landslide victory. David and I watched the international broadcast as hundreds of thousands of South Sudanese, joined by dignitaries from around the world and millions watching the telecast, gathered to commemorate their very first Independence Day and the birth of the earth's newest nation. The Republic of South Sudan, as they have chosen to be called, celebrated their "birthday" on July 9—which also happens to be David's birthday. God, I keep learning, is full of surprises!

I've heard that weeds spring up quickly, but big trees grow slowly. An effective prayer life is forged through perseverance over time. It's important to give your best energy to daily work, rather than surviving from crisis to crisis. I'm reminded of Paul's prayer in Ephesians 3:17, 18: "I pray that you, being rooted and established in love, may have power, together with all the saints, to grasp how wide and long and high and deep is the love of Christ." That's my prayer for you as you continue this journey.

PART FOUR

Agree with Others in Prayer

Chapter 7

Teammates

If two of you agree down here on earth concerning anything you ask,
my Father in heaven will do it for you. For where two or three gather
together as my followers, I am there among them.

—MATTHEW 18:19–20, NLT

It has been said that you are only as happy as your unhappiest child. I learned how very true this was about two years into my prayer experiment in 2003. Our oldest son, thirteen-year-old David (DB, as we call him) had severely dislocated his knee playing basketball. Fervent prayer took on a new meaning for me.

Feeling overwhelmed with emotion for my hurting son, I realized I needed help. It was then that I discovered the enormous power of partnering in prayer. Beth had raised five football players. All her boys were high school standouts, earning scholarships to play for The Citadel, Army, and Appalachian State. Beth and her husband, Gene, it seemed, knew how to produce strong boys.

I called Beth to see if she would join me in praying for my son's healing. I was full of fear for DB and needed support. DB was just thirteen but six foot one at the time and still growing. Since he was a young boy, his dream had been to play basketball in college like his dad. What about his growth plates? I agonized. Would he ever walk normally again and could he play the sport he so loved? I knew I couldn't carry this burden alone. There is something special about having two moms join forces in what I can only describe as "mother bear" prayer.

WHEN TWO AGREE

Thus began our prayer partnership, which continues today. I soon discovered that this petite, cheerful mom was part princess and part warrior! She was as tenacious in prayer as she was effervescent in personality. For years, Beth had relied on prayer as her secret weapon—her parenting tool of choice. After our son's injury, she became a lifeline.

During the crisis with DB, Beth reminded me that in 1 Samuel, David and Jonathan continually encouraged each other as prayer partners. "Cheer up!" Beth would say. "We have entrusted each other and each other's children into the hands of the Lord" (Jonathan's promise to David in 1 Samuel 18:42). The word *cheer* actually comes from the same Greek root as *courage* (*chardia*—"heart"), so this "cheerleading" mother was actually a courageous prayer warrior and just what I needed.

Jesus promised His listeners that "if two of you on earth agree about anything you ask for, it will be done for you by my Father in heaven" (Matthew 18:19). I learned that the Greek word for agreement is *symphone* (from which we get "symphony"), meaning "together with the same voice." This Greek word could also be translated as "music."

Beth and I "agreed" in prayer, first for our own husbands and children and gradually extending to those around us. Our fervent prayers of agreement eventually stretched beyond our own walls, into our community and even to a world thousands of miles away. In your own personal prayer experiment, I hope you'll reflect upon how you can bring the power of "agreement" into your prayer life. As you'll see, I think it's one of the most power-packed aspects of prayer. Having prayer partnerships will also sharpen your listening, your watching, and your ability to hear God, as I would soon discover.

Beth and I watched the news and read the paper, asking God for whom we should pray. Sudan, Pakistan, India, and Israel all made our "list." We shared our needs with "one voice," in agreement. I think when we join together in prayer, it must sound like music to God. I know I like it when my own children get along and act like they love one another.

Although I am still mystified as to why this seems to strengthen prayer, I know from experience that the prayer of agreement seems to ignite prayer with an extra power. Perhaps because Jesus promises that when we are gathered, even just two or three of us, in His name, He is there with us.

PRAYER FOR HEALING

Our son's injury was the sort that would drive a worrier like me crazy had it not been for prayer. What at first looked like a simple dislocation with a possible bone chip requiring a pretty routine arthroscopic repair turned out to require a three-hour surgery in which Dr. Glenn Perry, our orthopedic specialist, practically rebuilt our son's kneecap. In fact, the injury, in which it was discovered that most of our son's cartilage was sheared off the kneecap, was the first of its kind for this seasoned surgeon. He not only specialized in sports injuries but also was the personal physician of our city's professional basketball team. When it came to sports injuries, this guy was a pro. He was also our friend and had recently started attending our church—quite a step of faith for the self-proclaimed skeptic.

As Glenn tells the story, the knee injury turned out to be much more serious than he had thought—but there was a sliver of bone left on the cartilage. Could he dare try to reattach the bone? He suddenly stopped midstream in the surgery to pray for wisdom in performing the repair, a move that quite surprised his surgical team. They had never seen him pray during surgery. He then asked himself how he would proceed if it had been his thirteen-year-old son. After a long pause, he finally opted for a delicate reattachment of this tiny bone chip about the size of a nickel. His hope was that the vital cartilage attached to it would grow back to the kneecap. It was a long shot—he had not seen this kind of procedure performed. But if successful, it could allow many more years of sports for our son.

The anxiety, of course, was in the word *if*. The surgery would be a success if the bone chip grafted back to the kneecap—not a sure bet. And we wouldn't know for several weeks. In the meantime, our son would have to be in a straight-leg immobilizer so that the knee would be perfectly still during this time. No activity, no jostling, and no quick answers. We were forced to wait.

Beth and others continued to pray in agreement with us for DB's healing. A friend in the medical field even sent a note saying he and his family were praying for the "osteoblasts" to reattach. We were glad to have a few medically savvy friends among our prayer warriors! Still, the wait was agony. My prayers during this season were propelled by desperation.

An MRI was scheduled for ten weeks after surgery to see if the bone chip had reattached. Now doctors, by necessity, are realists.

But when Glenn called with the MRI results, I could tell his voice had a lilt in it. The radiologist, it seemed, was amazed by the results of our son's MRI—you couldn't even see the line where the bone had grown back, he excitedly told our surgeon. In other words, you couldn't even tell that it had been broken! The radiologist had sounded like a "kid in a candy store" when giving Glenn this wonderful news. I am convinced prayer made a difference.

The straight-leg immobilizer could come off and the hard work of eight months of rehabilitation could begin. During DB's rehab, Beth wrote him a letter of encouragement. One of her sons had battled through a similar injury but eventually returned full strength to the game. "Trust Jesus and work hard in rehab," Beth wrote. "I am praying you will play stronger than ever."

One day when clowning around on his crutches, DB lifted himself up on the couch in kind of a hop step. He didn't know that I had been camping on a verse from the Bible, "But for you who revere my name, the sun of righteousness will rise with healing in His wings. And you will go out and leap like calves released from the stall" (Malachi 4:2). I knew in my heart, one day he would be leaping and playing ball again.

Even the grueling rehabilitation process had purpose, and led to an incredible determination that served our son well as he diligently pursued his dream to play college basketball. He would eventually grow to his full stature of six foot nine and about 220 pounds of sheer muscle. No doubt my prayer life also became more muscular through that incredibly tough battle—but it was not over yet.

Prayer on Demand

Beth had an amazing heart for anyone and everyone who needed prayer. It could be the lady who worked in the bakery section of our local grocery store, the mother of one of her children's friends, or someone halfway around the world. Beth would listen to news reports and read the papers, searching for clues as to how to pray.

It seemed like we were always on the go. Our laundry load, with seven athletes between us, was near flattening. Our prayer pattern had to fit the flurry of our days in order to work. With so many family members and problems between the two of us, not to mention the crises in the world, prayer needs could arise on a moment's notice. Who can "gather together" each day, or even find time to talk on the phone?

Thankfully, cell phones are a great way to leave a quick message, which Beth and I called our "Prayers on Demand," or PODs for short. A quick POD message or text could quickly alert the other to pray for the pressing need of the moment. Sometimes, we would just leave a verse or a word of encouragement. I continued to refer to my urgent prayers as "PODs" and added new PODs to my Chubby Book list as needed. The POD signal spread among our friends; almost daily now, I receive a POD alerting me to drop what I'm doing and pray.

We began to share our lists, and it was common for us to leave each other a quick voice mail. "POD for the president of Pakistan. Remember we have been praying for him on Fridays. He just survived an assassination attempt." Or "Let's pray for our next-door neighbors. Their son was just deployed to Iraq."

Beth and I developed a special heart for our men and women in uniform. One morning, I read in the paper about Chip Stevens (not his real name), a Charlotte FBI agent who was leaving for Iraq to be in charge of U.S. intelligence during the early stages of the war. It would be a delicate and dangerous operation. I felt a need to pray for his safety, so I called Beth and we began to pray for Chip.

Beth and I prayed often for this man and his family. We knew he carried a huge weight of responsibility and faced danger on a daily basis. I had never met the Stevenses, but we had mutual friends, so I called Chip's wife one day just to let her know that Beth and I were praying for her husband and their three daughters.

Chip came home safely after several weeks of intense activity and a number of "near misses." God, we were sure, had kept him safe. Neither Beth nor I had a chance to meet Chip or his family until an unusual serendipity occurred two years later.

Beth called me one day and asked, "What was the last name of that FBI agent we prayed for a few years ago? It wasn't Stevens, was it?" One of Beth's teenaged sons had begun dating a young lady whose last name was Stevens. And, you guessed it. She turned out to be Chip Stevens's daughter. Just think—we had prayed years earlier for this very girl while her father was on assignment in Iraq.

The couple continued to date through high school and the families became the closest of friends. What started as a simple connection in prayer gave birth to a great celebration when the two became engaged to be married over Christmas several years later! Beth and I are convinced that this wonderful blessing began with our prayers for protection of a then-unknown FBI agent, serving his country on foreign soil. When two agree in prayer, there is great power. And if those two are praying moms, look out!

Prayer for Our Dreams

It's one thing to entrust your trials into the hands of a prayer partner. Most people are eager to join with you when trouble hits. I don't know why, but it is harder for me to entrust the dreams of my heart to another person than it is my troubles.

One of these special heart's desires was for my daughter, Bethany.

When she reached high school, Bethany changed to a private school that was known for its excellent French department. She had spent most of her ten years of public school in a French immersion program and was nearly fluent in the language. Moving to an elite private school as a sophomore was a challenge.

Though she knew no one when she entered, she found the school welcoming and a good fit for her gifts and talents. She made lots of friends and flourished on the volleyball and basketball courts. The school was a good fit academically and socially.

But as her senior year began, she decided to take some lonely stands, rather than follow some of her friends in the drinking and partying that is so much a part of high school life for many of today's teens. *Was it really worth it to stand for God and follow His less-traveled path?* she wondered in lonely moments.

David and I hurt for her and prayed for God to find some way to allow His favor to shine upon her and bring encouragement. One Friday morning after our usual pastor's day-off ritual of coffee and prayer time, we got the call. Bethany was shocked and amazed to learn she had been selected as a homecoming semifinalist. As she put it, she "wasn't even on the radar screen" for this distinction.

I called Beth for prayer, excited but a little tentative. Would she be willing to pray with me for Bethany to be voted to the homecoming court? It seemed like kind of a lightweight prayer. After all, we had been praying for a world at war. Besides, I know that we as parents sometimes compete against each other when it comes to our children. Would Beth even "want" to pray for this honor for Bethany? I'll never forget her response.

"Homecoming court?" she exclaimed. "Why, we are going to pray for her to be the homecoming queen!" I'll always treasure the gift from Beth that day as she rejoiced and wanted the dream with me. That kind of agreement taught me a lesson about both prayer and love. One of the greatest gestures of love you can give to a friend is to want the secret dream she holds dear in her heart with her.

Just a week later Bethany was crowned as homecoming queen, surrounded by her cheering friends. David and I sensed that God had done something very special in the life of our daughter. Continuing to stand firm in her faith, she used the open door to encourage others to live for Christ, bringing kingdom impact to the blessing we believe was from God.

Since that magical night, numerous mothers have confided to me that Bethany's willingness to stand tall, and sometimes alone, for Christ gave their daughters courage to follow a path that honored God. Better yet, Bethany is convinced God entrusted her with this special answer to prayer on her behalf.

Beth and I have continued to pray fervently for God to guard our children's dreams. We have come to believe that God uses those dreams to draw young people close to Him. Their dreams can open doors for them to make an impact for Christ in this broken and hurting world. Mother Teresa's words ring true: "Tread gently around the dreams of a child. You may be treading on the dreams of God."

Not everyone sees our child's dreams as clearly as we parents can. David and I prayed early and fervently for the treasured dreams of our children. I believe God gives parents, and especially mothers, an instinctive ability to see and believe in our children's dreams.

We are told that "by faith," Moses's parents had the courage to hide him from the genocidal king (Hebrews 11:23). Why? Because they saw "he was a beautiful child." The word in the Greek Bible for *beautiful, asteios,* is used only once in the entire New Testament. It means elegant, sophisticated, artistic, courtly, and a city dweller.

That's quite a package for two Hebrew peasants to observe in their baby—and yet it was the perfect combination of attributes to equip the young Moses to be raised in Pharaoh's courts. Surviving a mass killing, drifting in a basket in a crocodile-infested river, and growing up Egyptian were just some of the obstacles Moses overcame on the road to his destiny as Israel's deliverer. I'm certain Moses's mother prayed for her child's dreams as only a mother can.

Though our husbands playfully labeled Beth and me the "mad scientists of prayer," we knew they saw the results. And when your teenagers start asking you for prayer, you know you are on to something. Over the years, we began to build our own history of seeing God at work. Beth and I learned what it means to "have each other's backs." We will readily admit that when it comes to prayer, it's crucial to spend lots of time alone with God, growing strong and fit in our individual faith walk. But to go the distance, and to experience a synergy of power in prayer, we'd agree: Don't try this alone!

Prayer in Combat Boots

I thought I knew a thing or two about praying fervently for my children to overcome challenges to reach their dreams until I met a few single mothers in tough circumstances. They were true prayer warriors for their children. Jackie showed me what can happen when a faith-filled mother in a fragile neighborhood prays for her children to reach their dreams.

Our boys were basketball teammates throughout high school. Jackie and I would talk in the stands during games. Pretty soon, though we were different in many ways, we realized that we had this in common: we were two moms praying hard for our children's dreams. Jackie prayed fervently for DB during his injury. I prayed for her daughter Shona's seemingly impossible dream of going to medical school—quite a stretch, since no one in her family had ever gone to college.

College counselors tried to steer Shona to a more "realistic" goal, perhaps a small nursing school. But Shona persevered, and Jackie prayed. "I was discouraged and ready to give up," Shona tells the story. But one day her mother said, "Shona, don't you know WHOSE you are? God is in control, not man. Delight yourself in the Lord and He will give you the desires of your heart." Shona adds, "Well you can't argue with that, can you? I got into medical school!"

Talented and determined children like Shona, fighting hard-hitting obstacles, along with some especially courageous praying mothers, convinced me that there's no power on earth like a praying mom. R. A. Torrey, the author of *How to Pray*, tells of his wayward years when he was wandering far from God. Once Torrey awakened in the middle of the night and surrendered his life to Jesus Christ. "As far as I can remember," he writes, "I had not the slightest thought of being converted when I went to bed. But I was awakened in the middle of the night and converted probably inside of five minutes. . . . I was about as near eternal perdition as one gets. But I had forgotten my mother's prayers."[1] Like my husband says, "If you have a praying mother, you are toast!"

Praying mothers, I discovered, are relentless warriors when praying for their children's dreams. Two or three mothers agreeing in prayer for one another's children equals turbocharged prayer. I would soon learn that when the storms of life hit hardest, it helps to have a prayer army.

PRAYER POWER IN A TEAM

Our daughter's college roommate, Terri Lee, was dating a young marine who had just served two tours in Iraq. Over lunch one day,

Steven commented that he, like any good marine, is always on alert, even when in civilian settings. "I can usually tell if someone is a potential threat—even at Walmart." He grinned.

He proceeded to tell me about a marine's trained response when disaster occurs. "First," he said, "we are trained to run toward, not away from, the danger. Second, I say to myself, 'Where are my men?'" I wondered if this was to make sure his men were safe and accounted for. Steven answered, "No, it's because I know I cannot do this by myself." One of the purposes of boot camp is to teach a marine that he must function as part of a team for his own survival.

The Apostle Paul knew the importance of teamwork. "Join me in my struggle by praying to God for me," Paul urged his fellow believers in Romans 15:30–32 as he faced dangers and hardships in his work for God. The word for *struggle* is *synagonizomai*, from *syn*, meaning "with," and *agon*, or a "struggle, contest, or fight." Paul was asking his friends to agonize with him in prayer. Soon, I would be asking friends to agonize with me in prayer, too.

We got the call from DB's school on a quiet Friday afternoon. DB, by now fifteen, had injured his other knee in a freak accident at school. A few of his basketball teammates were playing a pickup softball game, trying to stay loose as they waited to travel to an out-of-town game. Coach Faulkner, his beloved basketball coach and also his PE teacher, tossed DB a pitch.

As he swung the bat, DB twisted to hit the ball. He suddenly crumpled in a flash of pain as his knee dislocated, shearing off cartilage in what we would soon learn was the identical injury he had suffered on the other knee. It was almost two years after the first injury—to the day!

David rushed to the school to take him to our doctor. Coach Faulkner was badly shaken—he cared about all his players, and knew how hard DB had worked to regain ground after the previous knee injury. I was devastated, and wondered how our son could make it through this ordeal again.

That same afternoon, as I was preparing to meet DB at the surgeon's office, I learned that my mother suffered a near-fatal ruptured appendix. I rushed over to help my dad at the hospital, keeping an all-night vigil with them after her emergency surgery at 2 a.m.

David and our son were in one emergency room, and my dad and I were with my mother in the other. I know what Paul meant by "agonizing" in prayer. In addition to this load, we were ending the long struggle David's mother had suffered with Alzheimer's disease. She died just two weeks later.

Somehow, I managed to keep my morning routine of running and prayer—it was my survival secret during this incredibly stressful time. My running buddy, Susan, who had been a constant encourager throughout DB's first injury, could tell I was barely holding it together one morning during our run. The second injury plus Mom's crisis were too much to bear.

After listening to my burdens as we rounded the last leg of our early-morning jog, she observed, "You know, basketball is a team sport. Maybe you need to depend on your team of prayer warriors for this one."

Beth, Susan, and others served as a team who literally prayed us through those difficult days and weeks that followed. I'm so grateful there were others willing to struggle with us in prayer for our son and my mom. I had seen the value of prayer partnership—this time I was seeing the power of team prayer.

The crisis passed—Daddy never left my mother's side during her arduous recovery, changing bandages and caring for her around the clock with an endurance that amazed even their nurses. And somehow, DB made it through the surgery—same as the last one—and another eight months of rehab. He dug down deep within and emerged from the experience with a strong commitment to his sport and even stronger character. We watched as his faith in Christ grew. James 1:2–4 became life verses for him. "Consider it pure joy, my brothers, whenever you face trials of many kinds, because you know that the testing of your faith develops perseverance. Perseverance must finish its work so that you may be mature and complete, not lacking anything."

Our son became a man before our eyes. In time, he returned to play for both his high school team and the AAU circuit. He would make it onto the college recruiting radar as a power forward, with over twenty Division One basketball scholarship offers. As for me, I'm both reminded and sobered by how much I need a team of people to join me in prayer. As my marine friend said, when disaster hits (or even on normal days), I look around and say, "Where is my team? I can't do this by myself."

A PRAYER TEAM FOR THE WORLD

The Bible calls this kind of prayer the "prayer in one accord." Whenever such prayer is mentioned, it is always accompanied by larger-than-life results. Praying with two or three people about the same need is powerful. Praying in unity for the same need with a group of like-minded believers is sheer combustion.

When the early believers met in the Upper Room, waiting for the promised Holy Spirit, we are told that they "joined together constantly in prayer" (Acts 1:14). When the Holy Spirit comes upon them in Acts 2, we are told the room shook with power. In Acts 12, Peter was in prison awaiting certain execution. "But the church was earnestly praying to God for him" (Acts 12:5). The results? The prison shook, the chains fell off, and Peter walked out a free man, accompanied by an angel (Acts 12:7–10)!

When others joined with me in my personal prayer needs, I could truly sense a lightening of my heart. It's a mystery as to why group prayer gives extra power, but even researchers at Duke University Medical Center acknowledged that patients who had people interceding for them in prayer got well faster than those who didn't.[2] I don't know why prayer in one accord has power—I just know that it does.

If team prayer could help me carry my own prayer burdens, surely that same power would be crucial in praying for the needs of the world. Around five years into my prayer journey, in 2006, I had a strong desire to gather a group of like-minded people who also had a heart to see Gospel impact expanded all over the earth. Forest Hill Church was starting to explore missions work in Central Africa and we needed God's guidance about where to send our people and resources.

I began with a few tried-and-true prayer veterans. Eager to pray, we called ourselves the "Women at the Well." There was an old well right outside the room where we met on the church property, but we drew our real inspiration from the woman at the well in the fourth chapter of John's Gospel; she had an impact on her entire community after a life-transforming encounter with Jesus (John 4).

The Women at the Well took prayer seriously and met weekly at noon to pray for the needs of the families, the church, the community, and the world. June, our South African friend, had seen God work in amazing ways over the years in response to her fervent devotion to God's Word and prayer, and both she and my prayer partner Beth were eager to share their trade secrets in prayer.

Jan had also been praying for years. This stylish but feisty grandmother brought equal measures of fervor and fun. I once heard her remark that we should be the kind of women who upon waking in the morning cause the devil to say, "Oh crap! She is awake!" Jan is also a devoted student of the Bible and one of her preferred prayer methods is to find a promise that seems to be just for her, and then "to hold on tight and don't let go." Jan is another "warrior woman" with a track record of answered prayer. No wonder her friends and family are always asking Jan for prayer.

Christina, my husband's ministry assistant, had also become passionate about prayer for the Sudan. She had seen an article in our local paper about a Charlotte resident, Cindy, who had traveled to the Sudan to make a documentary exposing the horrors of human slave trade there. Christina decided to contact Cindy, who agreed to share her story on my husband's weekly radio show. This was an important stepping-stone that eventually led to our trip to the Sudan with the Sacks of Hope.

Several months later, when we took the Sacks of Hope trip, Christina found herself on a plane, traveling with our group to the Sudan—quite a daring journey for a first-timer to Africa! Christina amped up the Women at the Well's prayer for that region as she became a passionate advocate for God's suffering church in the Sudan. She has recently completed her second mission trip to that region. Over the next five years, more and more ordinary people from Forest Hill Church would become involved in both short-term and career missions work in Central Africa.

I moved on to help launch another prayer group, but almost weekly I still receive a POD (prayer on demand) from these faithful prayer warriors for the world. The group now meets on Mondays and Thursdays at noon, and has grown to include a few men, too.

Who knows the scope of their impact? They intercede faithfully for the families in our church and community and the world beyond. I am convinced that their fervent prayers paved the way for the first steps of our church's work in the Sudan and Central Africa.

As you've been reading about the power of the prayer of agreement, I hope you've taken some time to ask yourself how you, too, can find team support in prayer. Do you have a prayer partner? If you are married, the first person to consider is your spouse. I could write another chapter about the power of the prayer of agreement in my marriage and family. The old saying "the family that prays together stays together" is true. Begin now to share your prayer list with your family. Even if some of them are not believers in Christ or the power of prayer, I encourage you to let them know which day of the week you pray for them. The results may surprise you. Beth and I knew we were on target when our teens began calling us with their PODs—for exams, sports, even life decisions. You're building your own family history and a memorial of God's work in your lives, and you can't do it alone. You need a team.

PART FIVE

Arm Yourself with Spiritual Strength

Chapter 8

Temple Upkeep

So I run with purpose in every step. . . . I discipline my body like an
athlete, training it to do what it should.

—1 Corinthians 9:26, 27, NLT

I've always loved sports—so it naturally follows that I admire
athletes. As I mentioned, I am married to a former college basketball
player, and I've been mother to our volleyball player, Bethany; our
basketball player, DB; and now Michael, our swimmer. Through
a relatively heavy involvement with sports over my lifetime, I have
realized that there is much to be learned about my spiritual life from
observing the personal disciplines of these athletes.

The Apostle Paul must have loved sports, too. He likens the
life of faith to the hard work of training for a sport. "I run with
purpose in every step," he writes. "I discipline my body like an
athlete, training it to do what it should. Otherwise, I fear that after
preaching to others I myself might be disqualified" (1 Corinthians
9:26, NLT).

Instead of the word *discipline*, I learned through my concordance
that some translations use the word *buffet*, which means "to treat

roughly." During my last annual checkup, our physician sounded a little like the Apostle Paul when he encouraged me to stick with my early-morning running routine. "Whatever you are doing, Marilynn, keep it up." Without knowing it, my doctor seemed to echo Paul's advice to treat the body a bit "roughly" when he quipped, "Stay mad at yourself." He was right. I'd personally rather be a couch potato. But I've learned that it helps to stay a little bit "mad at myself," so I will continue to buffet my body through exercise. Keeping a rein on my flesh in this way helps me stay alert and self-controlled for the purpose of prayer.

The word *buffet* came even more alive for me last summer as I watched our youngest son, Michael, along with hundreds of high-ranked swimmers from all over the state compete in the championship meet. Considering the grueling hours of practice involved, it should come as no surprise that these athletes were "buff" in every way. Finely chiseled muscles bore witness to hours in the pool, hours with weights, hours of running, all for the love of the sport. With a bodybuilder, the goal is . . . the body. But for a swimmer, the body is a tool. The great physique is not for show—rather, it enables these kids to swim incredibly fast.

Sports provide such a great metaphor for the training necessary to develop the habit of continual and effectual prayer. It's not that prayer itself is always hard. Often, it's like breathing—an ongoing conversation with God. But to stay alert, mindful, and available to listen—this kind of prayer can be challenging in a busy, noisy world. And carving out time to read God's Word and pray takes discipline and commitment. This doesn't happen easily and it doesn't happen overnight.

We've already discussed how persistence in prayer can be trying—especially when we are in pain, when all we can see with our natural eyes looks hopeless, and when answers are slow in coming. No wonder Paul tells the church in Colossae about his friend Epaphras. Paul told them that behind the scenes, this guy was continually "laboring" (*agonizomai,* from which we get *agony*) in prayer for them (Colossians 4:12, 13).

Daily, I get to watch an up-close and personal example of persistence as our son Michael pursues his passion of swimming. For a swimmer, practice can be repetitious, exhausting, sometimes agonizing. Ask any swimmer. There are competitions when you feel stuck, with no progress—your personal times don't budge. But then there are those breakthrough meets, those special races, when times are shattered, records broken. These are the rewards for all the work and daily practices. Why do these kids train, and train, and train some more? For the love of the race. Why do we pray, and pray, and then pray some more? For the love of our God, and commitment to the race He has set before us.

THE SPIRITUAL BATTLE

It strikes me that despite my generally gentle personality, I often use athletic, sometimes military, images when talking about prayer. I guess I'm in good company. In Paul's second letter to young Timothy, he compares the Christian life to that of a "good soldier," "an athlete," and a "hardworking farmer." My family tree is full of all three—soldiers, athletes, and farmers—including my own dad, who is one of the few remaining World War II submarine veterans. (David's family, incidentally, is made up of mostly ministers. His father, his brother, his uncle, and a family of six great-uncles were all preachers. Honestly, did the guy think he could really run from the ministry?)

And perhaps I developed something of a warrior spirit during my battle with infertility (which I'll tell you more about in Chapter

9). The fight of faith during those days has given birth to a certain tenacity in my spirit. And now as a mom, it's true; I continue to pray like a mother bear protecting her cubs.

This fierce love for my family gives me a glimpse of how much God loves us. It's because He so desperately loves His world that He "sent His only son," we are told in John 3:16. The verse also reminds us that without Christ there is a worse fate, a "perishing." We're in a spiritual war against the powers of darkness.

"There is a devil," said R. A. Torrey. "That's why we pray." If you asked me why it's important to bring order and discipline to our lives for the purpose of prayer, I would simply say, "Because we are in a spiritual war." "Put on the full armor of God," advised Paul, "so that you can take your stand against the devil's schemes." The struggle, he reminds us, is a spiritual one (Ephesians 6:11, 12).

The battle we fight, largely, is to sustain this habit of daily prayer. Our "spiritual house" may be threatened in a fast fight with the devil, but the day-to-day work we do to keep the thing clean is what makes us most useful to God in the spiritual battle that constantly wages behind the scenes (Luke 11:24, 25). Spiritual maintenance doesn't sound as dramatic or exciting as spiritual warfare, but it's vitally important to our daily victories in prayer. It's the daily grind of keeping your spirit strong that works not only as an affront to Satan's destructive mission, but also as armor against it.

The events of 9/11 stripped the illusion of safety and peace from America's mind. We now know that we will probably always be at war with terror on this earth, and spiritual battles are always looming as well. The Bible admonishes us to live daily as sober and alert, because "the devil prowls around like a roaring lion, looking for someone to devour" (1 Peter 5:8).

Anyone with combat experience will tell you that alertness

and preparation, along with mindfulness to details, can make the difference in victory or defeat, life or death. Our oldest son, DB, attended a military academy in Virginia for one year after high school to play for their top-ranked prep basketball team. He and his teammates banked on the fact that though it was sure to be tough, this experience would help them become bigger, faster, quicker, and stronger ball players. The school's success in launching college basketball players spoke for itself.

But life at a military academy is not what you'd exactly call fun. DB would never tell you he liked being in full dress, at attention, and ready to march by 6 a.m. Nor did he enjoy the strict discipline and what seemed like freakish attention to detail. His shoes had to be lined up to an exact inch from the wall. The sink could have no toothpaste traces, and his bed had to be made with absolutely no wrinkles—all before the sun came up. Some cadets even slept on top of the already-made beds, and threw an extra blanket over them at night, rather than face an imperfectly made bed, subsequent demerits, and the hours of marching around the bullring that were sure to follow. Oh, and did I mention the buzz cuts? But at the year's end, our son's training paid off and he headed off to fulfill his dream of playing Division One college basketball.

Other cadets headed for West Point or the Naval Academy, and some eventually to combat. Over its hundred-year history, the school has sent scores of young men off to fight, and many to die, defending our nation's freedom. A sign displayed on a campus wall at my son's academy prominently displays the Revolutionary War quote: "The price of freedom is eternal vigilance."

The Bible encourages us to be vigilant in guarding our spiritual freedom. We are reminded to pray constantly. Yet life moves at such a fast pace. Sometimes we forget to guard that line of communication with God. I learned the same lesson again and again, that listening to prayer works best when I am alert and self-controlled. This, in turn, makes me more sensitive to God's daily marching orders. That, I believe, is the role we play in the spiritual war: we must keep our spirits strong. It's what I like to call temple upkeep.

YOUR SPIRITUAL LIFE PATTERN

A person who decides to follow Christ will figure out pretty quickly that there are struggles with the world, the devil, and our own human nature, or what the Bible calls "the flesh." Paul knew that the battle had to be fought on all sides. I learned that by paying attention to my daily habits, my use of my time, and my priorities, I could form a daily pattern—even more specifically, a routine—that made room for prayer. I call this my "life pattern." Put simply, it's a way of arranging your days so that you've consciously factored in time with God. And it's essential to temple upkeep.

"No discipline seems pleasant at the time, but painful," the writer of Hebrews tells us (12:11). "Later on, however, it produces a harvest of righteousness and peace for those who have been trained by it." The human body, though an amazing piece of equipment, is still earthbound and subject to all kinds of desires and propensities to get off track. We must take charge of it, so it doesn't control us.

The solution? I found I had to take steps to stay solidly connected to Jesus throughout my day. It's about a relationship, but as in any relationship, it's helpful to have a plan. We grow in that relationship with Christ when we align ourselves to God's Word through the guidance of the Holy Spirit.

When it comes to your life pattern, I encourage you to take some time to think about how to build structure, rather than a rigid schedule or daily checklist. God has created you with a wonderful combination of spiritual gifts, talents, personality traits, goals, and dreams, even life experiences that should be reflected in how you order your days. And think about your energy. Are your best hours, your "power hours," in the morning or the afternoon? How much rest do you need to stay strong? When it comes to humans, one size does not fit all. I can take a pattern and alter it to fit me. The Bible exhorts us to holiness, and conformity to Christ—not to one another. And while there are basics we will have in common, my life pattern will look different from yours.

My daughter recently had her first baby. When Anna Grace was a newborn, Bethany's hours were consumed with nursing and caring for her precious baby girl. It was a round-the-clock job. For her, times with the Lord had to be sandwiched in between feedings, changing diapers, bath times.

My young friend Shona works ninety-hour weeks in her medical school residency at a low-income clinic. She's lucky to find time for sleep, much less long hours of Bible study. This is a season for her that's vastly different from mine.

The three of us share a love of Christ, of prayer, and of listening to God's voice daily. But our seasons of life, and even our gifts, talents, life experiences, and personalities vary. An effective life pattern must reflect our differences.

I've shared a sample spiritual life pattern on the next page. Take some time to think about your own structure. How do you spend your days? What are your priorities? When are your most effective hours of work? It's been estimated that 80 percent of your best impact comes from 20 percent of your work. How does your structure help or hinder your habit of prayer? Your personal health? Your home life? Your ability to be quiet enough to hear God's voice? You might want to use your journal or notebook to experiment with forming a life pattern.

SAMPLE DAILY LIFE PATTERN

✦

My first hours of the day, or my power hours, are my most effective. I devote those to my morning launch and my high-impact work. The daily focus in the afternoons, however, remains flexible. Sometimes a day needs to be switched around, or canceled completely. The key to a good pattern is keeping your life balanced. But I'm pretty ruthless with the day off. David and I carefully guard Fridays, our "Sabbath."

5:15 to 8 a.m.: Morning launch

- Outdoor run with buddy Susan
- Time in God's Word and prayer

8 a.m. to noon: High-impact work

- Writing
- Study
- Message preparation

Noon to 1:30 p.m.: Refueling time

- Lunch (sometimes with family or friends)
- Reflective reading
- Rest (a power nap?)

1:30 to 5:00 p.m.: Daily focus*

- Varied: meetings, errands, etc. (see opposite)

5 to 8 p.m.: Evening routine

- Dinner preparation
- Homework

8 p.m.: Quitting time

- Family time
- Wind down before bed

*Daily focus (1:30 to 5 p.m.)

Mondays—Thursdays: work, meetings, shopping, errands, etc.

Fridays: David and I take our Sabbath—breakfast out, rest, prayer, family time!

Saturdays: sports, home chores, kids' sleepovers, swim meets

Sundays: worship, family time, recreation

In my journey to learn to hear God's voice, I've added a morning run, time in God's Word, creating a prayer list, joining with my husband in prayer, agreement with a prayer partner, the Chubby Book, and the Study Bible—all tools and tips I've found useful along the way. Putting this together on a daily basis, however, plus going about my life, can be challenging. I found that a framework like this life pattern was so helpful to keep prayer front and center during my busy days. I not only wanted to follow hard after God, I wanted stamina to go the distance and finish my Christian race strong. It became clear that a balanced life pattern was a key to sustainability.

I try to carve out time for prayer and God's Word and give my best hours of the day to the work God has called me to do. The rest of my activities seem to fall into place when these high-priority items are in order.

The Physical/Spiritual Connection

Plenty has been written about lifestyle management and how this pertains to daily structure. But I want you to consider how this applies to prayer. Our physical and spiritual lives are connected. Just ask anyone who has suffered depression. The Bible even calls your body a "temple" for the Holy Spirit.

You've heard it all before, and I don't want to be another source of guilt for you. But it's unavoidable: if you want a strong spirit, keeping your body healthy is important. It's worth the effort to put some energy into staying physically healthy. You get only one body, and, as the phrase "temple upkeep" hints at, our bodies actually house our spirits. Surely it's reasonable, even obvious, that if one is unhealthy, the other probably is, too? They're interconnected.

So, take the time to consider if you get enough exercise. Studies have shown that 150 minutes of aerobic exercise a week over a thirty-day period can raise your serotonin levels as much as an antidepressant. Translated, that's just thirty minutes of fast walking or jogging five days a week. Cutting back on white flour and sugar and loading up on fresh fruits and vegetables, whole grains, lean meat, fish, and plenty of pure water will also make a difference in your physical health.

And while you're at it, be careful what you feed your mind. A friend of ours is waging his own brave battle with cancer. He carefully guards what he eats. But he's also noticed that it's important to watch what he puts into his mind. Even too much mindless television watching can weaken his sense of well-being. In his fight of faith, he's learned to be vigilant on all fronts.

Another friend in an alcohol recovery program has learned to be careful what she feeds both her body and her brain in her personal battle with addiction. Those in the recovery community know the mantra. "Before you drink, HALT!" Are you Hungry, Angry, Lonely, or Tired? That's when you are most vulnerable to relapse. Don't fight alone, they are warned—call a friend!

Paul must have seen the obvious connection between our mental health and what we put into our minds. He follows his instructions on dealing with anxiety in Philippians 4:6, 7 with a pithy training tip on how to guard our minds. "Finally, brothers, whatever is true, whatever is noble, whatever is right, whatever is pure, whatever is lovely, whatever is admirable—if anything is excellent or praiseworthy—think about such things" (Philippians 4:8). There's your mental diet manual in one easy sentence.

Paul reminds us in the next verse to "put into practice" the things we've learned from him, with the promise that the "God of peace" will be with us (Philippians 4:9). It matters what you feed your brain if you want to be strong for battle. David's mother used to say, "Garbage in, garbage out." It doesn't get any clearer than that!

People sometimes ask my advice about seeking therapy when they feel overwhelmed by life's problems. I encourage them to first try a little "temple upkeep," practicing these principles for thirty days, and then get counseling for what's left over. It's a whole lot cheaper that way!

TIPS FROM SAINT BENEDICT

It has been said that when the student is ready, "the teacher will appear." Some of my best lessons in the value of "training my temple" for prayer came from a sixth-century monk known the world over as Saint Benedict. Benedict and his group of followers were simply believers who attempted to keep the fires of their Christian faith alive amid the surrounding moral depravity and spiritual decay of what came to be known as the Dark Ages.

Their fight of faith was against ignorance, poverty, disease, and the spiritual corruption that raged throughout Europe. They devoted their lives to prayer, the study of Scripture, education, service to their community, work, and practical living. Acutely aware of the surrounding spiritual darkness, Benedict often encouraged his followers to remain alert and watchful for the "prowling enemy." They often slept in their clothes to be ready for the middle-of-the-night prayer battles that often ensued as they wrestled with these forces of darkness. Some credit Benedict and his followers with the preservation of Christianity. Others say that all of Western civilization owes its survival to those early spiritual warriors who came to be known as the "Benedictines."

Benedict challenged me to achieve a rhythm and a readiness in my ordinary days and nights that was both balanced and sustainable. Sustainability over the long haul had become my priority, along with prayer—and Benedict had some tried-and-true training tips. The "Rule of Saint Benedict," as it came to be known, has brought order and sanctity to daily life for many throughout the centuries that followed.[1]

Unlike other monastic groups of his day who thought spiritual progress could only be gained through harsh forms of self-denial and asceticism, Benedict stressed order and balance. He encouraged his followers to stay rested and well fed. He knew that his soldiers had to remain strong to prevail in battle.

All of life is sacred, believed Benedict. Every aspect of daily living was important to God, so Benedict helped his followers create a structure where prayer and listening to God could flourish. So could relationships, education, work, rest, service, and even recreation. Benedict also knew that this balanced life equipped his followers to face the many challenges facing them as they went full force against the spiritual and moral decay threatening the Dark Ages.

Since all of life mattered to God, believed Benedict, the sacred was not separate from the secular. Work was sacred along with one's spiritual disciplines. Benedict gave attention to the creation of a home environment and one's surroundings, as well as the rhythm of one's days. Listening to God's voice and prayer, he believed, could happen all day long, even while his followers were busy with the tasks of life.

As I continued to develop a daily pattern, my days gradually took on more stability and consistency. I began to realize that the hours in my day all belonged to God. No more "Now I am with God for my devotional—now I am on my own time." Prayer and listening to God flourished.

REMEMBER THE SABBATH?

Unlike many of his ecclesiastical contemporaries, Benedict saw much value in rest, teaching his followers to get a full seven or eight hours of sleep a night. This probably was a welcome relief to the typically sleep-deprived monastics of that day, who were known for sleeping just four or five hours.

Keeping the Sabbath was important, too, to ensure well-rested, creative, and balanced followers. There is a reason God talks so much about the importance of a day of rest. He devotes as much attention to Sabbath-keeping in the Bible as He does idolatry. It's that important.

Staying rested and taking a day off are crucial to temple upkeep. This, in turn, makes us better prepared for prayer and more alert for spiritual battles. As a wise pastor observed after watching one too many fellow clergy leave ministry because of moral failures, ministers can "exhaust themselves" into moral failure if they ignore the need for rest.

David and I have long valued our day off together. Since weekends are workdays for both of us, we take Fridays as our "Sabbath." Recently, when asked to list our top ten tips for a successful marriage, we both, without knowing how the other would answer, listed "taking a day off together each week" as our number one tip. As my husband often says, "If you are burning your candle at both ends, you are not as bright as you think!"

Carving out a little rest on a daily basis, however, was new turf for me. But I learned eventually, and I give Saint Benedict all the credit. He indirectly taught me how to take a really great nap. Actually, he didn't talk specifically about napping, but rather what he called taking breaks in the day for "rest and reflective reading." I decided to set aside about an hour after lunch to rest. The rest became especially important for me when my days began before daylight. I needed to remain alert for the final carpool round to pick up my son after evening workouts.

Humans, I discovered the hard way, are not built to do quality work for sixteen hours straight. Even an attorney would count eight highly concentrated hours of work, or "billable hours," a good day. What made me think I could work straight through a long day without a break?

So if I wanted to be armed with spiritual strength, I needed to learn to rest. A nap was a welcome addition to many days. My good (and very hardworking!) friend told me her play-by-play approach to a good nap: "One must remove shoes and socks, and get under the sheets," she explained. "Then, set the alarm for a wake-up time about an hour later, and begin reading." I almost always fell asleep . . . but never so long as to be groggy. Voilà! Truly, this was the perfect power nap. I awoke alert and refreshed. And over the long haul, this kind of "temple upkeep" made my prayer receptors sharper throughout the day. I was more likely to be ready for whatever challenges I faced in my day. Plus, I was just plain nicer to be around.

If it seems like I work hard at prayer, it's because I believe prayer works. Or rather, God works through our prayers. My morning launch, the list, prayer triggers, and watching for answers throughout the day, along with PODs sent by Beth, family members, and friends—all keep my mind attuned to prayer and listening to God. Conversations with God have become constant running commentary. I find this a much better task for my mind than worry. Perhaps this is what it means to "pray without ceasing."

I want to be useful to God to pray for His world—a world in trouble. I want to be powerful and effective in praying for family, friends, and neighbors. And I want to go the distance. It has been well worth the effort to "train myself to sustain myself" so I can finish strong.

But what happens when we get discouraged or weary, or when we feel like we can't take another step? When we hit bottom, does our prayer life go with us? To the contrary, we may find that God whispers a secret. It's when we're broken that He gives us His *best* treasures. His mightiest power is reserved for our times of weakness. You may discover, as I have, that this is really good news.

Chapter 9

Strength in Weakness

"My power is made perfect in weakness" . . .
for when I am weak, then I am strong.

—2 CORINTHIANS 12:9, 10

My greatest lesson in power-filled prayer did not come, as I would have expected, through a balanced life pattern, or training tips, or discipline, or even fervor. My greatest lesson in prayer came, instead, through weakness. The paradox of receiving spiritual strength when we are at our weakest is a concept that I continually find hard to grasp. And yet, biblically, I can't get around it. In looking back over the decades I've followed Christ, it's clear that the greatest works of God in my life have come when I was at the end of my own human strength.

I've talked about how Elijah's prayers inspired me as I embarked on my journey in prayer after 9/11. Elijah was known for his strength and his zeal. He prayed powerful and effective prayers. But as I had learned, it was during a time of utter defeat that Elijah had his most powerful encounter with God.

Years ago the Lord had steered my life way off course from my original plans. Who could have imagined I would give up a corporate career to marry a minister? And you might assume that someone who marries a minister is a sure bet when it comes to hearing from God. Yet my early years were spent trying to run away from God's voice. I remember learning about the Christian faith from my parents and even had a childlike awareness of God's presence. But the years slipped by and my heart toughened as I began to listen to other, more compelling voices. I was aware of a hunger, a God-shaped void, as the French philosopher Pascal called it. But I just wasn't sure God could be trusted with my life.

So a curious dance developed between God and me. I pursued life, goals, excitement, achievement, fulfillment. Yet all the while, I sensed that God was steadily pursuing me. By the time I reached high school, I reflected on the social landscape with its adolescent pecking order. It was obvious. If God was your main voice, there was a pretty good chance you'd end up a loser. And so at around fifteen, I told God in no uncertain terms that I preferred to face life on my own.

I accumulated an impressive string of academic honors, found myself in lots of leadership roles, and was twice voted campus homecoming queen—in high school and later at the University of Georgia. It certainly looked to me as though taking charge of my own life had been a smart choice. I gradually stopped believing in God.

Once during my agnostic years, I was home from college visiting my home church with my family. As I listened to the minister's sermon, I thought to myself, *I can't imagine a bigger waste of a person's time and talent than becoming a preacher.* I distinctly remember this afterthought: *except being a preacher's wife!* That thought would come back to haunt me.

God's voice continued ever so softly to whisper to me. And when crowns had lost their luster, relationships had soured, goals proved empty, and I was thoroughly sickened at who I had become, God was quietly waiting for my return.

A pastor friend put a copy of C. S. Lewis's *Mere Christianity* into my hands.[1] It sat on my shelf for a year. While home from college on summer vacation, I began reading. Piece by piece, page after page, Lewis, himself a former atheist, dismantled every argument I had carefully constructed to shut God out of my life.

I began to see that my entire life had been built on a subtle form of performance and pride. These, Lewis argued, rather than the more obvious kinds of evil, were actually Satan's preferred strategies. To this day, I'm not quite sure why Lewis's logic found its mark so completely, but on the inside, I was shattered. *Oh, no. This guy is right and this is the truth. I have been following the wrong path.* I sat stunned. Here I thought I had been an atheist, but the realization hit me. *I have actually been a student of the devil.*

I felt the full weight of conviction—I knew I was guilty. I also knew I had to make a choice. Right at that very moment, on that hot summer day in Georgia, August 8, 1976, sitting beside our neighborhood pool, I quietly gave all I knew of myself to all I knew of God.

Though I was sure this decision would result in the certain death of every hope and dream I'd ever known, my surrender resulted in relief—and the beginning of a new life and better dreams.

Just a year later, I met David. Some friends set us up on a blind date. I immediately fell in love with this tall, handsome, kind-hearted basketball-player-turned-preacher. We married within the year. So much for my vow to never marry a minister.

WHEN YOU BREAK, WHERE DO YOU RUN?

Now here I was, years later, trying to learn secrets about prayer from an Old Testament prophet. I continued to study Elijah's story even after 9/11. I knew there was much more to learn. In reflecting back over the events of my life, I realized that God had taken me through my own training ground. Like Elijah, I had come face-to-face with my brokenness.

I had seen a statue of the prophet Elijah when visiting Israel years earlier. The sinewy fireball of a man looked more warrior than prophet. After praying for God to bring drought as judgment upon faithless Israel, he gave a whipping to the evil mob of pagan prophets in his own "Super Bowl of Faith." The feisty prophet then climbed to a mountaintop to pray for rain—and ran the distance of a full marathon to beat Ahab back to Jezreel in time to await the downpour (you can read the full story in 1 Kings 18:22–46).

Yet, after all that, when faced with retaliatory death threats from Ahab's wicked wife, Queen Jezebel, Elijah had a serious meltdown. "Terrified," we're told in 1 Kings 19:3, Elijah "ran for his life." The self-described "zealot for God," the steely iron-man-triathlete of faith, had exhausted himself into what we would call a clinical depression. "I am ready to die," he told God. He felt alone and utterly defeated—as broken down as the rest of Israel.

But herein lies the secret: when Elijah broke, he knew where to run. Elijah ran to Mount Horeb—the place where he knew he would encounter God. And what did God do? Fed him, put him to sleep, fed him again. Only after this period of intensive rest and refueling did the Lord speak to Elijah.

This time, God was not in the earthquake, wind, or fire, but rather in a gentle whisper. And in this intimate conversation—humbled yet renewed after his time of utter brokenness—Elijah saw a new side of God, and probably a new side of himself. Though fervent in faith and mighty in strength, Elijah had discovered the full extent of God's great love for him during his time of greatest weakness. When you break, where do you run? It's during these times of absolute breaking that you become most receptive to God's voice, most willing to receive His strength.

MY OWN ELIJAH DAYS

The events of 9/11 took my prayer to new depths, but desperate prayer was not unfamiliar territory for me. I reflected on how a few years earlier, I had experienced my own time of personal brokenness during a long and grueling battle with infertility. Up to that point, my recipe for success had pretty much been the same: if you want something, just set your mind on the goal and don't stop working until you reach the prize.

Eventually, after a couple of years of marriage, David and I began looking forward to the day when we would have children. Imagine my dismay when our hopes for a baby stretched into six months, a year, two years, and eventually four years—forty-eight straight months of drugs, temperature charts, surgeries, tests, tests, and more tests. And still no baby.

Exhausted, I wondered, *How long can I endure?* I was desperate. If you have experienced infertility, you know what I mean. Those struggling to have a child are reported to subject themselves to incredible medical extremes, surpassed only by terminal cancer patients. It's as if a primal survival instinct kicks in, willing you to keep trying to find an answer.

Tests had shown that I suffered from a condition known as endometriosis, which can cause infertility. This resulted in severe abdominal scarring, which had impeded pregnancy. Medical procedures thus far were unsuccessful—I began to realize that even medicine is an inexact science. I explored natural healing, nutritional therapy, and other means of aiding conception. And, like Elijah, I ran to God.

Now when you get really desperate, you'd think it would be instinctive to go to God. But this is when faith is truly tested. "This problem is too important to leave with God," says the voice of the tempter. "Better take things into your own hands." I think that's how some people fall into addictions and idols—running away from God instead of toward Him in their pain.

But I had already tried life without God. I had given it my best shot, only to realize I was hopelessly lost. I had surrendered myself to Christ by the pool that August afternoon a few years earlier. I held nothing back—He had all of me. Where else could I go?

Strength came as I rested in God, studied His Word, and listened for His voice. I scoured the pages of Scripture to keep my hope alive. I discovered that the Bible had numerous stories of barren women, all desperate for God. They valiantly fought the fight of faith, and eventually bore children. What's more, the children born to these barren women included some real "Hall of Famers" of the faith. Practically everybody who was anybody in the Bible was born to a barren woman—Isaac, Jacob, Joseph, Samuel, even John the Baptist. I found allies in Sarah, Rebecca, Rachel, Hannah, and Elizabeth, inspired by all the prayer that went into their times of waiting. Their stories gave me hope. I grew to believe God would give us a baby—but I also knew we might have to wait. And so I waited—and waited.

Not getting what you want when you want it may be one of the best tools for sharpening your hearing of God's voice and for strengthening your faith. Notice I didn't say not getting what you want at all. I find that people are more easily able to dismiss their heart's desire altogether than to wait. Sometimes it's easier to give up in defeat and walk away from a dream entirely than to stand on God's promise, clinging to the hope God has placed in your heart.

That's why waiting on God is such an incredible test of faith—I refer to this time in my life as "wait training." And just as physical weights make our bodies strong, I learned that "wait training" forged my spiritual strength. By holding on to God's promises and persevering when things seemed hopeless, I experienced a surge of the Holy Spirit's power deep within.

I fed myself on the promises of God's Word about healing—too many to count—day after day, month after month. During those "Elijah days," I learned to hear God's whispers of encouragement, trust His character. In short, I learned the secret of what Jesus meant when He said "abide in me" (see John 15:4). The fight of faith was making my faith strong in ways I couldn't see at the time.

We had enlisted the help of a highly recommended doctor— friends had told us of his remarkable success with hard cases like ours. In our first consultation with the specialist, he reviewed my records from a previous surgery. Looking at the report, he said it appeared that not only did I have abdominal scar tissue, but my fallopian tubes were actually scarred shut from the endometriosis. He was not optimistic. I went numb. Scarred shut? I had remembered scar tissue being mentioned, but nothing about the tubes being scarred shut. "I'll try to laser out the scar tissue, and if possible, save a tube," I barely heard him say amid my fog.

David and I looked at each other. How had we missed this? And how does one open a tiny tube (about a centimeter in diameter) that is completely scarred shut so that a tiny egg can pass through? We left the office deflated and confused.

Yet we continued to draw strength from each other and from the conviction that we both believed we heard God encouraging us to press on and not give up hope. Looking to the biblical example of Abraham and Sarah, I purposed in my heart to keep believing. *Even if I am old, like Sarah,* I whispered to God, *I will still keep believing Your promise. Despite what the facts tell us, I still believe You have placed this dream for a baby in our hearts. It's now in Your hands. I believe I have heard Your voice, but I trust You no matter what.*

We scheduled major abdominal surgery for six weeks later. A peace beyond description enveloped me. "You'll never know Jesus is all you need until He is all you have," Mother Teresa once said.

I felt close to God and somehow shielded from worry. Two nights before the surgery, I was channel surfing and happened upon a Christian television show. A bit skeptical, but also curious, I listened to the pastor. He had his head bowed and was praying for healing of various ailments. "And there is someone out there struggling with"—he paused as if searching for the right words—"struggling with scar tissue. I don't know if it's around the area of their heart—no it's scar tissue in their abdomen." He added, "God wants you to know you are healed."

Scar tissue in their abdomen—who could possibly care about scar tissue in their abdomen except me? That is for me! I pulled out my journal and noted the time, date, and words, carefully writing all the evidence in case this startling scenario proved true.

I checked into the hospital the next afternoon, with surgery scheduled the following morning. The surgery, we were told, could last up to four hours, during which time they would use laser technology to attempt to repair and open the fallopian tubes.

Forty-five minutes into the operation, the surgeon called my husband for an immediate consultation. David was afraid it meant bad news. *Had they found something awful and simply closed her back up?* He feared the worst.

Meanwhile, I awakened groggy in the recovery room, with a man in a white coat peering over me. He had red hair and a very kind voice. "You did really well in surgery," he said gently, his face near to mine. "Your tubes are perfect," he whispered. Deeply comforted, I dozed back off.

David was in his own conversation down the hall with a perplexed surgeon. The fallopian tubes, which had been scarred shut, were now perfectly normal. The tubes were not simply improved—they were perfect.

David greeted me as I came to, and before he could say a word, I whispered, "I'm healed, aren't I?" I just knew it. I began inwardly rejoicing as he smiled. Strangely, no one remembered seeing a red-haired man in a white coat in the recovery room, but I know he was there. I've wondered if the mysterious man with the kind voice was really an angel, a messenger with good news from God.

It was still six weeks of recovery following the abdominal surgery. I had such peace as I waited. During those days, I almost felt like I was "expecting." I even bought a baby carrier and began to paint the nursery in anticipation. The first month we could try, we conceived our Bethany. I took the page from my journal documenting the healing prayer to our surgeon. He and his wife became dear friends and began attending our church—their own faith encouraged by our miracle. A year later we went back to the same floor of that hospital, this time on the maternity wing, where Bethany entered the world to the cheers of so many of the staff who had cared for us before.

Combined with the additional times of waiting for our two boys, I calculated that I spent about ninety-six months of waiting for babies—I like to think it's the equivalent of a PhD in wait training!

POWER MADE PERFECT IN WEAKNESS

The lessons during those days of waiting had trained me to hear God's voice. I learned to stay linked to Him through faith, rest, and humility when my own strength fell far short. Humility is a constant companion when you are desperately waiting for something. Dependency on God makes you realize just how small you really are. Strangely, I found that brought freedom. With an awareness of my frailty came an awareness of the incredible strength and power of God.

The Apostle Paul discovered this same aspect of God's grace during his own times of trial. He had pleaded with God to take away what the Bible calls a "thorn in the flesh," some weakness or affliction that Paul said "tormented" him. But the Lord comforted Paul with these words: "My grace is sufficient for you, for my power is made perfect in weakness." Paul eventually got to the point that he welcomed weakness and hardship and could even say, "when I am weak, then I am strong" (2 Corinthians 12:10b).

As a wise friend once remarked after weathering multiple family tragedies, faith still intact, "Control is just an illusion." And despite all the tools, tips, personal discipline, and strategies for prayer, I keep learning the same lesson—some of God's most amazing work occurs when I am flattened by life.

If you are going through your own times of weakness and discouragement, I hope you will pause and reflect. What might God be saying to you? You may find, as I did, that during your pain, you're most sensitive to the voice of God.

Our times of weakness don't repel God or wreck our prayers. In fact, God's grace shines brightest through our broken places. You may have crash-landed into the end of your own strength and have nothing to bring to God but the broken pieces of your life. I believe that if you will trust Him, you will find that His strength really does work best when you are weak.

And while you are waiting for healing, for victory in your trial, for the answers to your own prayers, I encourage you to lift up your eyes and look around you. Is there someone who is going through a time of pain—his or her own Elijah days? Have you considered that maybe you have just the love and tenderness needed to lift the burden of another? You can begin with prayer. As you continue to move forward in your own prayer journey, don't leave your broken moments behind. Bring them with you.

Your times of brokenness could be the most valuable thing you bring to your personal journey in prayer. It's there that you may discover the secret of real strength. You may be on the brink of seeing your mess become your miracle. For it's when we are broken that we're most likely to be used by God.

PART SIX

Answer God's Call

Chapter 10

Lift Up Your Eyes and Look

Go! I am sending you out like lambs among wolves.

—LUKE 10:3

I'll never watch *Hotel Rwanda*. At least that's what I told the friend who suggested I see the movie, knowing my heart for Africa. The film's portrayal of the Rwandan genocide was graphic—I didn't need a movie to show me what I knew to be a frenzy of tribal killings.

Yet here I was, in Rwanda, standing in front of the actual Hotel Rwanda, or Hotel of a Thousand Hills, as it is known to Rwandans. I was looking at the very building where the courageous hotel manager, Paul Rusesabagina, sheltered his own family and more than a thousand fellow citizens during the genocide.

I couldn't imagine this beautiful country piled high with dead bodies and with rivers of blood, but that is how my friends in Rwanda describe those dark days. Nearly a million Tutsis and moderate Hutus were slaughtered in a killing spree that lasted ninety days, beginning in April of 1994. That was a fourth of Rwanda's entire population at the time. I remember *Time* magazine's chilling cover with a missionary's quote: "There are no devils left in hell. They are all in Rwanda."

CHANGE OF HEART

If I'm honest with myself, I have to admit that I would not have chosen to go to Rwanda. It was not on my list of places to see before I died. In fact, the prayer journey I began seven years earlier on 9/11 was initially more about prayers of protection for my own family and my country than it was about praying for the needs of the world. But over time, prayer had made my heart more receptive to the world beyond my own. That same year, 2008, I had visited the Sudan. I've shared some of that story and how for the first time, my eyes were opened to the horrors of genocide. Now, here I was again, in yet another genocide-torn region of Africa. What was God doing?

I had asked God to narrow my search as I continued to pray for a hurting world, never dreaming I'd go to Rwanda. If God had a list of countries that burdened His heart, I imagine Rwanda would be near the top. I was here with a team from Forest Hill who were visiting Rwanda and her nearby "twin," Burundi. We were exploring how our church could be part of God's work in rebuilding this war-torn region. We represented a variety of ages and stages, but the fourteen of us shared a common yearning: How could our lives make a difference? What was God calling us to do here in East Africa, a region ravaged by decades of civil war and genocide?

Our journey was born out of a year of focused prayer and seeking God together to hear His heart. Prayer with a group of like-minded people is powerful, truly the church at its best. This kind of prayer has inspired every great missionary movement, starting in the book of Acts and extending to modern missionary movements of today. Historically, the church's mission to spread the Gospel to the lost and the least has been sparked and sustained by prayer. Our team had been praying about what this mission might look like, and now our boots were on the ground.

We were here at the invitation of Dr. Célestin Musekura, founder and president of African Leadership and Reconciliation Ministries, or ALARM. Célestin was the first Rwandan I'd ever met. He knew the ravages of war firsthand—members of his own family had been brutally murdered in a mass revenge killing after the genocide. Gripped by a burden for his homeland, Célestin sensed God calling him to help bring forgiveness and reconciliation to the people of Rwanda, which for Hutus and Tutsis had to begin with reconciliation with God. So much killing had occurred—everyone in Rwanda, it seemed, was in need of forgiving or being forgiven.

Our church had donated funds to some ALARM projects, including a secondary school for genocide orphans. We were there to see where our dollars had gone and explore new projects. ALARM equips teams of ordinary men and women to teach pastors, government leaders, women, and children as part of their Bible-training program. But Célestin also wanted us to understand the heart of his people. Relationships are key—and Americans have much more to offer Africans than just their money, Célestin explained.

And Africans, he assured us, have much to teach Americans. We could learn much about perseverance through what they have suffered, and especially how they survived. We would be also encouraged by their strong faith in Christ, Célestin promised. He said it would be a mutual exchange. How right he was.

Sometimes God Roars

It was Charles's story that shattered any superficiality in my practice of listening to God's voice. Something about the encounter with Charles forced me to dig deeply into what I believed about the character of God. When it seemed as though evil had triumphed in

Rwanda, could I still hear God's voice of love? Several of our team went to a small church known as Nyamata, the site of the massacre of more than five thousand terrified men, women, and children who had packed the church sanctuary for days, seeking refuge from the roving bands of government militia and frenzied citizens.

The hand-scrawled sign outside, "Never Again," was as much a prayer as a reminder. Nyamata was not a sanitized memorial. The smell of death was real and raw as we stepped inside the small church. Piles of blood-soaked clothing and shoes, thousands of skulls, bloodstains, and bullet holes testified to the unspeakable horrors that occurred that spring day nearly fifteen years earlier. Remains had been identified by loved ones and carefully put in boxes that bore the names of the victims. Nyamata stood as a silent memorial to that dark day.

Our guide Charles, a soft-spoken, attractive young man in his early twenties, was the sole survivor in his family of ten. He had been a nine-year-old boy during the massacre and an eyewitness to the gruesome events. He took us through the church, stopping to explain what happened during those six terror-filled hours.

I was struck by the calmness in his tone as he stopped to point out bloodstains on the walls. "Here is where the soldiers grabbed babies and little children by their ankles and dashed their heads against the walls."

Charles described other unspeakable acts of cruelty—the killing was not quick. We were left shaken and silent. Eventually one of our team members, Joan, with the sensitivity of a wise counselor, gently asked Charles if he would be willing to share some of his own story. How, she wondered, was he able to be one of the very few to make it out alive?

Charles paused a minute, and then began to give us a deeply personal glimpse into how, as a nine-year-old, his world exploded that day. "Here's where I lay on the floor and played dead," he pointed. His eighteen-year-old sister, Charles explained, had been raped and after having had one arm cut off, threw herself over her little brother.

A soldier had decided to simply shoot instead of torture her, so mercifully, she died, but not before she whispered to Charles to lie still and play dead. So the nine-year-old, with rivers of blood around him, lay among the bodies for several days. He finally made his way out and wandered in the marsh area in a stupor for weeks. Somehow, Charles had survived. I carefully studied his face. His was not the face of a shattered man. Somehow, he had gone on to live life and find love and purpose.

Suddenly, the Rwandan genocide wasn't about a million faceless victims in a forgotten land halfway around the world. It was about one—and he had a name and a face. Charles was standing in front of me. He had once been a little boy, like any little boy. He would have been like my Michael, who at age nine would have also had a big sister, eighteen. What if it were my Bethany throwing herself on Michael to protect him? It was unthinkable. And it was real. Too real! Charles is just like me; the only difference is our geography. *God, why did you let me see this?*

Our group stood quietly around Charles—shaken but honored that he had entrusted us with his story. Célestin put his hand on Charles's shoulder and asked if we could pray for him. No one had done that for him before, Charles remarked. I wondered if anyone had heard his entire story.

Charles had endured the unspeakable, yet he seemed to have found a way to go on with life. He hadn't lost faith. He was giving back to others, keeping memories alive, but moving forward—he had more than survived.

For days after returning home, I wrestled with God. I nearly lost sight of His goodness, His compassion. Was He real? Was He good? The words almost sounded hollow. As far as my limited human perspective was concerned, God had missed it with Rwanda. Like most anyone who has seen the aftermath of genocide, I was stricken by the depth of evil I had encountered. How could this have occurred with God's supposedly omnipotent hand in control? How far could His grace or mercy extend when hell was allowed to spill over into earth?

My anger churned. *How could you let people endure such things, God?* If I ever wondered about the depth of man's capacity for evil, it now seared my soul.

I couldn't help thinking of some of my Jewish friends. For the first time, I had seen a glimpse of the same kind of hatred that was behind the Holocaust.

A few days after returning, I happened to pick up Elie Wiesel's Nobel Prize–winning Holocaust account, *Night,*[1] sitting on my bookshelf. Maybe reading this would help me somehow understand the "why" behind genocide. It was a bad idea. Pretty soon, I realized I should not have tried to read it while so raw. Wiesel described his own experience in the Nazi death camps. At one point he watched speechless as infants and children were tossed alive into the furnaces. My mind exploded. Alive. I didn't realize they were tossed in alive! "Enough, God! I have had it," I inwardly cried out. "Where were You in Rwanda, and where were You in the death camps? . . . Babies and children thrown alive . . . into the furnace." I kept repeating the words "alive in the furnace" over and over to myself.

I put down *Night,* unable to read further, and picked up my

Bible. My daily reading happened to take me to the third chapter of Daniel. Three young Jews, probably teenagers at the time, refused to bow down to King Nebuchadnezzar. Furious with rage, he had the furnace heated seven times hotter. A furnace. These words arrested me. *Jews thrown into the furnace.* Apparently, the furnace was not new territory for God or His persecuted people. The fire was so hot, the text tells, that the soldiers throwing them in were killed. The three teens were tied up and thrown in alive.

Yet, astonished, the king jumped up when he saw the three walking unbound among the flames. "They aren't even hurt by the flames!" he shouted. "And the fourth looks like the Son of God." The three were released, and Daniel's account tells us that not a hair on their heads was singed, their clothing was not scorched, and they didn't even smell of smoke!

In that inner place where I have learned to hear God's voice, the following words came quietly but forcefully: *I have ways of comforting My people, even in the furnace, ways that you know nothing about.*

Like a low roar, the voice was stern but loving—not unlike a tone I would use with my own children. But I felt more comfort than rebuke. And my soul drank this in like fresh water after days of feeling scorched. I didn't sense God was minimizing or even explaining the depth of extreme suffering experienced by some of His children. Only that He was there. The fourth man in the fire. The man who hadn't been thrown in and shouldn't have been there was the Son of God. God incarnate, giving comfort in a way that I, thankfully, had never known, had never needed to know, and could not possibly grasp at that moment. Somehow, these words restored my assurance that God was real—He was loving, good, and in control. I was certain of His presence. And for now, that was enough.

BREAK MY HEART FOR WHAT BREAKS YOURS

My experience at Nyamata with Charles left me with the distinct impression that God had entrusted me with a precious gift. He had not only deepened my heart of prayer for the world but also had let me taste the sufferings of Christ. I could have continued my prayer journey half a world away, going about business as usual. But God allowed me to see why it mattered that I, as a Christian, am called to leave my place of comfort. He allowed me to see the world with new eyes so that I would answer His call.

Whether in Africa or down the street in our own neighborhood, broken people, desperate for the love of Christ, are all around us— sometimes we just don't see them. "Open your eyes and look," Jesus told His disciples in John 4:35. "The fields are ripe for harvest." In Luke's Gospel, He reminds them that though the harvest is plentiful, the workers are few. "Ask the Lord of the harvest, therefore, to send out workers into his harvest field" (Luke 10:2). The Greek word for *send out* is *ekballo,* the same word used when Jesus "cast out" demons. He seemed to know that sometimes we won't leave our places of comfort without a push! During my journey in prayer, I learned that when God moves us out of our safe places and back into the hurting world, He might just shake things up a bit.

When Lucy asked if Aslan (the allegorical Christ figure in the C. S. Lewis masterpiece *The Lion, the Witch and the Wardrobe*) was a safe lion, Mr. Beaver replied, "Who said anything about safe? 'Course he isn't safe. But he's good. He's the King, I tell you."[2]

God, I learned, though very good, is not always safe. And for those of us who are serious about hearing the voice of God, safe is not always good. Since meeting Charles I have been to this region of Africa two more times as part of Forest Hill missions projects. Our work at Forest Hill Church has expanded to include initiatives throughout Central Africa. The team of volunteers continues to grow as people from all walks of life feel called to be part of what God is doing among the least and the lost. It's hard to see the things we saw without being moved to action.

I am not exactly sure why God allowed me to hear Charles's story or to see the suffering in Central Africa up close. Perhaps it's so I will tell others what I have seen. Or maybe He knew that as a sensitive mother, I would weep with Him over the suffering of His children. Remember, I had prayed all along for Him to break my heart with the things that broke His. One thing I know for sure. I will never forget what I saw and heard that day. My comfortable world had ceased to be comfortable. The point of prayer was to stay connected to the Lord daily—of this I was still certain. But I now realized that it also meant I must be available to answer His call.

Like He did in my encounter with Charles, God sometimes speaks with a shout, and when He does, look out! God has repeatedly nearly shoved me out of my well-oiled routine so that I will take His message into the broken world around me. I believe, if He hasn't already, He will make sure you experience His shouts as well.

If we are daily spending time in prayer, reading His Word and listening to His voice, we're more likely to be alert, "lifting up our eyes" to look for the people who need His love. Our prayer must lead to action. *How should I pray?* becomes *What can I give?* followed by *Where should I go?*

Chapter 11

So What? So That!

My sheep listen to my voice. I know them and they follow me.

—John 10:27

Michael and I were swimming in the ocean a few years ago. Suddenly my ten-year-old son got this wide-eyed look on his face and pointed behind me. "What is that?" "That" was a shark, fin above the water, swimming not more than four feet away! It was gliding past us, parallel to the shore. It's amazing how quickly a person can move through waist-deep water!

I had to alert the other swimmers! For some reason, instead of screaming "Shark!" I ran along the shoreline, swiftly but quietly motioning to each swimmer to look at what was coming his or her way and to get out in a hurry. Almost by instinct, I knew that panic, or thrashing about in the water, could be deadly. The shark swam for about fifty yards before veering off into deep water, presumably still looking for his lunch.

Sometimes, when you need to deliver an urgent message, it's best to keep your calm and speak in a whisper. That was yet another lesson I learned that day in the car on 9/11. Amid the tumult in the world around me, I had heard not only God's roar but also God's whisper, guiding me away from the surrounding fears and calling me to pray instead.

SOMETIMES GOD WHISPERS

God's "inside voice," I discovered in this journey in prayer, is what He uses to get across some of His most important messages. Remember, God didn't use the earthquake, wind, or fire to communicate to Elijah. It was His whisper that brought comfort, restoration, and a renewed calling to the exhausted prophet. And when God draws people out of darkness and into a lifesaving relationship with Him, He often speaks in whispers of love. It's His "kindness" that leads us to repentance, Paul tells us (Romans 2:4). God whispered to me after I began paying attention to watchful prayer and listening for His voice. I got the distinct impression that He was saying, "Prayer is just the beginning."

God had a larger reason for this journey in prayer and a particular purpose for my being here on earth. It wasn't just about hearing His voice. I was to learn about prayer and hearing His voice so that I would do His will. My life, I realized one day, was either a "so what" or a "so that." If I took these lessons no further than answers to my own prayers and my own family's needs, so what? Why would they matter?

You may have heard that Jesus saves you from your sins. But have you ever thought about what He saves you for? You're not just killing time as you wait for heaven. God has prepared a unique job description for you when you enter this new life in Christ. He has given you all the gifts and tools you need to be part of His larger plan on earth. We are saved by grace through faith in Jesus. But we are saved and set free to take the good news to others.

There had been great value in my training ground of becoming more disciplined, more alert, and more watchful on this journey in prayer. God was teaching me how to pray and how to listen, as well as how to walk on a daily basis, to "lead a life worthy of the calling" (Ephesians 4:1).

But He also wanted to communicate to me just where I should walk. And while the tools and training tips helped me grow in my relationship with Christ, they were also preparation for doing His work. Hearing God's voice could not be separated from doing His will. The words for *listen* and *obey* are the same in both Hebrew and Greek (the languages of the Old and New Testaments). Prayer couldn't stay behind closed doors, and neither could I.

The word *calling* is closely related to the Latin word *voca*, from which we get *vocation*. It's also the word from which we get *voice*. I regret that we have lost the understanding of a calling when we encourage our young people to find their careers.

A failure to have a clear understanding of one's calling can lead to emptiness and even despair. I heard about a recent study of the Facebook generation, the sixteen- to twenty-four-year-olds who have grown up with social networking as the new normal. Despite the massive amounts of online and text communications, one out of three of the young people surveyed felt lonely. Another one out of three reported being bored. Loneliness and boredom can make a person vulnerable to depression, anxiety, and addiction. Many in the Facebook generation, it would seem, for all their technological know-how, have trouble when it comes to finding purpose. How I long for the next generation to grasp the concept of God's calling.

LISTEN FOR YOUR CALLING

God doesn't play favorites. He doesn't love one generation, ethnic group, or nationality more than another. "For it is by grace you have been saved, through faith—and this not from yourselves, it is the gift of God . . ." Paul says in Ephesians 2:8. Salvation by grace through faith is everyone's starting point for prayer. It's also the starting point for discovering your calling.

We are told that each of us is specially designed by God. So it only makes sense that He has given us work to do during our time on earth. Our unique calling is prepared ahead of time—just waiting for us to discover it, according to Ephesians 2:10: "For we are God's workmanship, created in Christ Jesus to do good works, which God prepared in advance for us to do." He even hardwired into each of us the necessary set of gifts and skills to fulfill His calling (1 Peter 4:10).

I find that God often starts the conversation with us about our life's calling through the dreams of our heart when we are just children. He seems to draw us to Himself through those dreams even before we know Him. Over the years I've noticed it's around age ten when many dreams spring up. Think for a minute about the dreams you had as a child. Is it possible that God was speaking to you through your dreams even then?

I discovered how to harness the energy of worry for the purpose of prayer. In a similar way, I learned that dreams, especially for those I love, also provide energy for prayer. In fact, I don't think that our God-given dreams can become realities without prayer. When our dreams are aligned with His Word, they point us in the direction of God's plans for our life—or our calling. I began to realize that my calling was simply seeing God's plan for my life through His eyes. This is how I personally define *vision*. It makes sense, then, that dreams would require prayer, and lots of it.

Pause and Reflect

So ask yourself this question: *Is my life a "So What?" or a "So That"?* Like I said earlier, *How should I pray?* becomes *What can I give?* followed by *Where should I go?* God tends to shake things up a bit when He wants to move us out of our nest. This was true with the early Christians as well. In Acts 1:8, the apostles were told by Jesus to wait for the Holy Spirit. After they had received His power, He said, they were to leave their safety zone. They were to take the radical message about salvation through Christ to Jerusalem, Judea, Samaria, and to the ends of the earth. By the eighth chapter of the book of Acts, we find them still doing church in Jerusalem. They were growing, but they had not gone. We are told that a "great persecution broke out, and the believers fled to Judea and Samaria." And they took the Gospel message with them. As a missionary friend of mine once said, "If you don't follow the command in Acts 1:8, you might find that God shakes you up with a little of Acts 8:1."

Maybe God has been stirring your heart, preparing you to move beyond your areas of safety. You sense He is calling you to step out. You're just not sure how or where or even what that looks like. Before I share with you more of where my journey in prayer took me—my "so that"—I want to make sure you understand one thing. Your journey and your destination will look vastly different from mine.

Why? Because everything about you—your gifts, your life experiences, your heart's desires, even your sorrows—are all unique. God's calling for you may be mysterious, but it won't be random. He uses who you are, who He created you to be, and the life you've lived—with all your joys and heartbreaks, even your mistakes—to prepare you for your assignment.

If you think it's too late, or you've missed your opportunity, I will remind you of those words I heard years ago in the night. God is Real and He is a Rewarder of those who diligently seek Him (Hebrews 11:6). So keep seeking Him—He will lead you toward your calling. And remember that He loves to restore broken things, even broken dreams. He's famous for giving "double for your trouble."

My "So That"

The prayer journey I began on 9/11 was initially more about prayers of protection for my own family and my country than it was about praying for the needs of the world. I seem to remember those early prayers being more along the lines of *Help! Lord, save us from the terrorists!*

But nations are made up of people with faces and families. Afghanistan, Pakistan, and Iraq all made my prayer list. *Lord, You said we should pray for nations, so I am praying for Your transforming peace.* I borrowed another secret from Mission India founder John DeVries's *Why Pray?* I imagined a huge spotlight of God's love aimed at entire countries. I prayed for the protection of Christians in those countries, for God to defeat the powers of darkness, and for the church in America to wake up and pray for a world in trouble. I was often reminded of the journal entry dated October 11, 2001, just a month after 9/11:

Confession:
Lord, I have not prayed and travailed for the suffering of Your people worldwide. My view has been so narrow. The great suffering among Your people in the Sudan is staggering. Show me how to pray, Lord.

God began to warm my heart for the Sudan and her people long before I ever set foot in the country, as I've shared in detail. "Sudan Sam" became my attempt to put a face on the nation. Who could have imagined I'd actually meet a "Sudan Sam"? And when the South Sudan voted for its freedom in a history-making referendum in 2011, I awakened in the middle of the night, worrying and praying for my Sudanese friends.

During my ten-year experiment in prayer, I would be jolted out of my comfort zone and into places in my own city and around the world that I never knew existed. Somehow, God had transformed the very places that scared me to death into places where I could see faces of dearly loved friends when I closed my eyes.

Looking back, it's not surprising that God would ignite my heart for the world when He called me to pray on 9/11. I already had a passion for evangelism and was committed to serving the poor. David had long been teaching the people of Forest Hill Church about the importance of taking the Gospel to our own "Jerusalem . . . Judea . . . Samaria, and to the ends of the earth" (Acts 1:8). Many of us were continually praying for God "to break our hearts for the things that broke His." We even used the SO THAT! slogan on thousands of blue rubber bracelets, the kind Lance Armstrong made famous. This was a daily reminder for our people to ask if their lives were a "So What?" or a "SO THAT!" Did *How should I pray?* lead to *What can I give?* followed by *Where should I go?*

What did surprise me were some of the immediate answers to prayer as I focused on the world beyond my own walls. Answers would practically spring up before I finished praying. I called these "hot prayers." We humans tend to stick with what works. For me, enough answered prayers kept coming to convince me that I was hearing God's voice.

One morning, I wondered to myself, *God, where on earth are Your people suffering the most?* Later, I opened my laptop and noticed one of those catchy headlines—"What are the ten most unhappy countries on earth? Click here to find out." It was as if God had sent me the article Himself!

Of the more than 190 nations on earth, Burundi was at the very bottom. I'd never even heard of Burundi, but it made my prayer list that day. David and I, along with many of our leaders, began to have a burden for this tiny country.

Despite long years of war, the people seemed to have a resilient hope. I learned that Burundi had suffered the same genocide as Rwanda. But the extremist regime remained in power, so the killing in Burundi went on for over a decade, when the regime was finally toppled in 2005.

Once again, we traveled with a Forest Hill missions team to Burundi. For the second time in a little over a year, God opened another door for David and me to meet with an African president. This time, we were taken to the private quarters of President Pierre Nkurunziza. Wearing a warm-up suit and tennis shoes, the former teacher and soccer coach was preparing to make his weekly Saturday-morning trek into the villages for community workday.

Soon after taking office, the newly elected president had promised free primary education to his people. This required everyone's help on Saturday mornings to build schools. Burundians are passionate about education. Children would rather go to school than eat, it seemed. For them, education equals hope.

The former head of the rebel forces, Nkurunziza had been badly wounded during the war and left to die on a riverbank. Hovering between life and death for weeks, he somehow managed to read through a pocket New Testament someone had given to him. There by the river, he surrendered his life to Jesus Christ. If allowed to lead his people to freedom, he vowed to dedicate Burundi to the Lord.

David took off his SO THAT! bracelet and put it on the president's wrist. Our people would be solidly behind his efforts, David assured him. Could one church make a difference in an entire nation? We'd sure try.

Later during our visit, our team watched as tens of thousands gathered for a joyful thanksgiving service, praising God for their hard-won freedom. They had big dreams for their tiny nation. Surely God must love these people to bring us all the way to Central Africa.

In the last three years, various teams from Forest Hill have become involved in everything from training Christian leaders, to planting churches, to building Christian schools. Our church has also been involved in the construction of a reconciliation center for ALARM, where church and government leaders from all over East Africa can come to be trained in the truths from the Bible and leadership principles. Our prayers came to a stunning conclusion when the president and his wife came to Charlotte and visited Forest Hill in September of 2011. Five years earlier we began praying for the country of Burundi—and now its head of state was preaching in our church!

I looked up at the stage, listening to the president speak from the platform where my husband preaches his weekly sermons. It seemed surreal. Once again, prayer and listening to God's voice were not about me at all—but rather about hearing who God had on His heart. The believers in Burundi had been crying out to God on behalf of their country. I have no doubt He had called us to be part of His answer to their prayers. And in so many ways, they were the answer to ours. As for my assignment, the calling to help bring the good news of Jesus Christ to a small nation with big dreams was a perfect fit.

CLOSER TO HOME

Answering God's call doesn't always mean going to Africa. You can discover plenty of needs in your own backyard. One morning on the front page of our local paper, I happened to notice an article about a promising young high school student with few resources but big dreams. His name was Quentin. He was just eight years old when he discovered an old upright piano discarded by a neighbor. He begged his mother for the piano. Brenda recalls telling him, "Quentin, if you can get that thing home, you can have it," never dreaming that he would find a church volunteer to help him drag it behind a van into his garage. Quentin began teaching himself how to play on the old, out-of-tune piano. Now as a high school senior, he had been accepted to college to study music. He needed funds.

I thought to myself as I opened my laptop that day that I'd like to meet this kid; maybe there was a way to help him get to college. This was more of a wish than a prayer—no sooner had the thought left my mind than I glanced at my e-mails. I opened one from David. He had forwarded me an e-mail from a young man seeking scholarship help. I gasped—the young man was named . . . Quentin.

During this time, I had become part of our church's task force whose purpose was to explore ways to raise Christian leaders in fragile communities. If you want to amp up your prayer for the world, try seeking God together with a team of like-minded people.

We decided to help Quentin with his education, knowing that

with his big dreams and heart for God, he was sure to have an impact on other young kids from at-risk neighborhoods. One by one, other young people with limited resources but big dreams—most often with praying moms—began to come to our attention. Through Forest Hill, we formed a nonprofit organization called Seeds of Hope.[1] Kids like Quentin and Shona were among our first Seeds Scholars. Shona now serves as a doctor among the poor. Another graduate works on Wall Street. Still another is a standout campus leader. One aspires to be an architect, another is a nationally ranked chess champion. And then there's the homeless kid from the Bronx with God-sized dreams, along with several bright young leaders in Africa.

We believe that with Jesus in their hearts and a good education, kids can change their communities. Poverty will leave their heart even before they can physically escape the conditions of poverty. Dreams in any language or neighborhood, I've concluded, matter to God.

You Can't Do Everything, But You Can Do Something

Your "So That" will look different from mine. I share these details of where my journey led me for one reason. Though God's calling is mysterious, I want you to see that it is not random. I had long been praying for God to burden my heart for people and places that were on His heart. I wanted to take the message of the Gospel to people thirsty for God's grace. And with my heart for education and my love of big dreams, it makes sense that I would be passionate about helping others reach their dreams. The words I once saw on a sign have proven true for me: "To reach your dream is fulfilling—but to help others reach their dream is sublime."

The Bible says that each one of us has been given a gift, and we are to use that gift to "serve others, faithfully administering God's grace in its various forms" (1 Peter 4:10). When you decide to follow Christ, you have a new vocation—that of taking His good news to the world. You may not be passionate about education or big dreams in quite the same way as I am. But if you will seek God through prayer, and listen to His voice, you have the chance to answer God's unique calling for you. Like someone once said in response to the overwhelming needs in the world, "You can't do everything, but you can do something." Ask God what that something, that "So That," is for you.

My son-in-law, Ryan, and my daughter, Bethany, are giving their lives to reach our youth with the Gospel. My friend Jen has a giant heart for homeless children. Laura, a single mom raising two sons, sensed God calling her to open her heart and home to adopt her brother's boys when he and his wife were jailed on drug charges. Yvette began a ministry to help parents in a fragile community in our city. Lisa is using her leadership gifts to help bring racial reconciliation to women in our community. Michele and Raina expanded our Seeds Scholars program to reach more students in our own community and Central Africa. John, with a corporate background and compassionate heart, has strategically invested resources and equipped our people to take the Gospel to the poor in our own community and around the world.

Others have taken on radical assignments in dangerous places. Ashley, a former Realtor, heard God telling her to "lighten her load." She sold her earthly possessions—feeling called to Central Africa— and followed God's "assignment" for her life. Jon and Kristi packed up their goods and three children so they could bring the Gospel to Ethiopian young people. Our friend Ryan gave up everything after reading a story about the Sudan, and now lives and works among villagers in the remote Nuba Mountain region. And instead of enjoying a cozy retirement, Howard and JoAnn work tirelessly to share the love of Christ in Ethiopia.

What is your gift? Where is your calling? People who need the love of Christ are all around you, beginning with your own family. Maybe God will whisper to you about the needs of your next-door neighbor. Would you dare to venture into fragile neighborhoods in your own community? And with more than 190 nations on earth, surely there's one that needs your prayers. Ask God to show you who is on His heart. Today. Now.

I encourage you to seek God first in His Word through prayer. Stay connected to Him on a daily basis. Then go about your business. And as you are going, watch. Train your eyes to be alert for God at work. Then listen for His whispers. *Where do you need me today, God? Who is on Your heart? How do I love my family, neighbors, community, and the world?*

Make sure you are part of a local church—the Christian life is not a solo journey. Gather a group of friends around you to explore God's calling together. Then watch what happens. Some people feel called to pray, others give, and others may hop on a plane and go. When you start praying for God to burden your heart for people that are on His heart, it's rather like asking Him to give you a drink from a fire hose. Amazing things begin to happen.

Sometimes God whispers. Sometimes God roars. I hope you are learning to hear the voice of God. He is Real. He is a Rewarder of everyone who seeks Him. He will give you double for your trouble. And He will be with you each step of the way as you continue your adventure in prayer. The world around us groans with the weight of suffering. There is much work to be done. Perhaps God is saying to you at this very moment, "I need your help." Will you answer His call?

Afterword

Behold, I am coming soon! My reward is with me . . .

—REVELATION 22:12

I surveyed the room around me as I sat next to the bedside of my father-in-law, Dr. Howard Chadwick. Husband, father, grandfather, friend, and mentor to many. Pastor, vocalist, scholar—he had lived his life well.[1] As he approached the end, he surrounded himself with his worn Bible, a few pictures of family, and some of his wife's beautiful painted china—those, a recliner, and a *huge* flat-screen television. This dignified and frugal man had been overjoyed with his recent purchase. He and my husband had always loved watching sports together—it's what he wanted as he grew more frail and bedridden.

"I don't know if I want to be there when the end finally comes," David confided, exhausted after spending most of the day at his dad's bedside. "I'm just not sure I can bear it." He had walked through the difficult last several months with his beloved father, watching this once-vibrant man gradually lose strength. Granddaddy Chadwick lay dying. We knew he would be gone in a matter of days.

At ninety-one years of age, with seventy years in the ministry, he left a legacy that had touched so many. We had watched this graceful and dignified man with a booming voice grow weaker and weaker after a serious fall two months earlier that shattered his hip and shoulder.

The children and grandchildren had traveled from near and far to share their quiet good-byes. Granddaddy expressed his love to each of them, having been both a nurturer and mentor to us all. The hospice team encouraged us to keep to a reasonably normal schedule, counseling us that for someone who knew God as deeply as Dr. Chadwick did, there exists the mystery of his "choosing" when he is ready to go.

"Dad," as I referred to my father-in-law, and I had always shared a special closeness. How I treasured the affirming words he had spoken to me over the years. I could always count on him to pray for the special needs that came with the challenges and joys of our active family. He would have been too humble to admit it, but in my eyes, he was a hero in prayer. We shared a love of learning and reading. We also enjoyed a penchant for detail. David's mother used to say to me, "You remind me so much of Chad."

The night before Dad died, I suddenly awakened in the middle of the night, alarmed and fearful. *Lord, please comfort him,* I prayed. *Don't let him die tonight and don't let him die alone.* Bethany had spent the entire afternoon with her beloved granddaddy, and I remembered her prayer that angels would surround and comfort him throughout the night. She even prayed there might be special "angels of music" assigned to him, since he loved to sing.

I continued to wrestle with my worries in the dark. For an agonizing moment, I was tormented with guilt. If *only* I had been with him more, done more for him, said more to him. I could hardly bear it. But then, in that quiet moment, I remembered the prayer strategy I had long been practicing for dealing with worry—turning my worries into prayers. So I reminded myself, "If you are *worried* about this, then *ask* the Lord to do something, and be *specific*." I thought for a moment, then prayed. *Oh, Lord, I just want him to know how much I care. And Lord,* I added, *I want to be there with him when he dies.* As I prayed, I found myself almost speaking to Granddaddy, himself, whispering, "Hold on. I will be there soon." I dropped off to sleep.

The next morning I went to Dad's bedside, joining his best friend, Wayne. David would join us later. We reflected on the many ways Dad had blessed our lives. "He was the best man I ever knew," Wayne said quietly. Nurse after nurse stopped by. They had watched him nurture his wife of sixty-five years through a long battle with Alzheimer's until her death, five years earlier.

We marveled at how Dad rebounded after this devastating loss. He continued to preach and drive his car, and even assisted David in performing Bethany's wedding ceremony. He invited his friends and family to what he called his ninetieth "birthday bash."

I reflected on how Granddaddy had cheered from afar as our youngest son, Michael, began to excel in competitive swimming. His last prayer project was for our son DB's college basketball recruiting process, a journey Dad enjoyed each step of the way. He couldn't have known our son was actually signing his official NCAA letter of intent to play Division One basketball that very morning—or could he?

Even as he lost physical strength, Dad continued to provide counsel, love, and wisdom as a pastor and prayer warrior for all whose presence he graced. One minister friend told me he went to visit Dad, intending to bring comfort to him. Before he left, Dad had prayed for this man's hopes and dreams, managing to belt out a few lines in his still-beautiful baritone of "To Dream the Impossible Dream."

I hoped he could hear us as Wayne and I talked about his impact on so many lives. Wayne had faithfully visited Dad on a daily basis, and was grieving deeply at the loss of his best friend. "I'm not looking forward to this. The end could be really hard for him," Wayne said. "I hope he doesn't suffer too much at the very end." He left for a quick lunch, planning to return later that afternoon.

I went to my car for a quick snack to tide me over. Then, back in the room, I pulled Dad's recliner close to his bed so I could be near his face. It looked as though I might be there for several hours, so I had brought my Bible, my journal, and my Chubby Book with me.

I noticed a book lying open on his bedside stand. Picking it up, I saw that it was a Baptist hymn book printed in 1956. It was opened to the old hymn "Sweet Hour of Prayer."

That's odd, I thought. *This book wasn't here yesterday.* Dad had been a Presbyterian pastor for seventy years, but his mother, who died when he was twelve, was a devout Baptist . . . the *only* Baptist we knew of in the family. Granddaddy used to tell of his beloved mother dancing around and singing hymns while she cleaned house. I am guessing she was singing Baptist hymns. But who could have left a Baptist hymnal? Sitting comfortably in Dad's big recliner, I reflected on the words of the old hymn written more than a century earlier. It was as if the words were written just for that moment, so I decided to write them down in my Chubby Book. I wanted to always remember these words when I thought of Dad's final hours.

Sweet hour of prayer, sweet hour of prayer, that calls me from a world
of care
And bids me at my Father's throne make all my wants and wishes
known!

I stopped writing, conscious of the fact that these words were
speaking to *me* . . . it was if God Himself were telling me that He
was there with us, and that prayer *really* mattered. Dad had known
this . . . it was his way of life. I continued to copy the words:

In seasons of distress and grief my soul has often found relief, and oft
escaped the tempter's snare . . .

I paused in the middle of the verse, aware that these words had
become my prayer. *Lord . . . these words are just for Dad. Let him*
go quietly, without any more distress or grief. I glanced over at his
face before copying the final line of the hymn. Suddenly, I noticed
the side of Dad's face was growing lighter in color, and then in an
instant it hit me—he was gone! Quietly, without struggle, in the
seconds while I was writing the words of the hymn, he simply *left*.

I sat stunned for a moment. *What do I do?* I looked at my cell phone
to notice the time. It was *exactly* noon, not 11:59, not 12:01. Somehow,
it seemed important to know this. The time was of special significance
for me, since for months, I had practiced the habit of setting my cell
phone to remind me to pray every day for a minute precisely at noon.
For a moment, I paused, saddened, yet amazed at how quietly Dad
had gone home—and right at noon. I went quickly to find his nurse.

As she moved swiftly to check vital signs, I quietly sat back
down in Dad's recliner and noted these words in my prayer

booklet: *Dad left peacefully at exactly twelve o'clock noon.* Then I picked up where I had left off, jotting down the final words of the hymn verse: *In seasons of distress and grief my soul has often found relief, and oft escaped the tempter's snare . . . by thy return sweet hour of prayer.* I was compelled to record every detail—to preserve the beauty of this moment. I knew I would then be able to assure my husband and the rest of the family that Dad had died peacefully and that he was not alone. The words of the hymn were somehow significant.

I asked the nurse if she knew who left the Baptist hymnal. "You know, I heard that someone was in here at midnight last night with the door shut, singing to him," the nurse said quietly. "Our night shift nurse is from Africa. Her name is Mary. She is very religious . . . maybe it was Mary."

Mary from Africa. I am still wondering how a nurse from Africa found a Baptist hymnal from 1956 and left it open to "Sweet Hour of Prayer." And what was she singing to him at midnight the night before he died at noon the next day?

Mary couldn't have known that Dad's own mother, the "good Baptist" in the family, died when he was just a boy. And that his precious mother loved to sing to him as she cleaned house. Perhaps she used to sing "Sweet Hour of Prayer." Perhaps she was singing it with Mary the night before her dear son came to join her. I'd like to think so. And I am so very thankful that God answered my prayer and let me be there for the moment.

Later that day, I looked in a collection of hymns and found the words to a final stanza of "Sweet Hour of Prayer" not included in the Baptist hymnal. Truly, these words must have described Granddaddy Chadwick's departure!

Sweet hour of prayer, sweet hour of prayer, May I thy consolation
    share,
Till from Mount Pisgah's lofty height I view my home and take my
    flight:
This robe of flesh I'll drop, and rise to seize the everlasting prize,
And shout while passing thru the air, "Farewell, farewell, sweet hour
    of prayer."[2]

I know that Dad is now with the Lord. He can finally see Him face-to-face. I am sure he is learning the answers to the questions we all have here on earth. As David is fond of saying, the word most often spoken in heaven will be "Ohhh . . . ," as we begin to understand things from God's perspective. Dad now understands the mysteries we can only see dimly. That's the reward that awaits all of us who journey to know the Lord during our time here on earth.

Going Deeper

Bonus Feature 1: Personal Reflection Questions

The questions here serve a double purpose. If you are meeting in a group, a portion of these questions will be assigned to you each week. If you are reading this book on your own, these questions will help you get the most out of your prayer journey. Consider working through them as you go through the six steps. Or share them with a prayer partner!

PART ONE: BE ALERT
Chapters 1, "Listen," and 2, "Keep Watch"
- How would you describe your prayer life: fueled by crisis or daily and powerful?
- What fear or worry is causing you to pray more fervently? What are a few things you've already tried besides prayer in order to solve the problem?
- How might you turn that worry into a prayer? Is there a verse from the Bible that gives you hope in this circumstance?

PART TWO: BE SPECIFIC
Chapters 3, "The List," and 4, "The Chubby Book Method"
- Is your personality more of an adventurer who enjoys a little chaos or structured and orderly?
- Reflect on the value of listing specific prayer concerns. Did the exercise of making the list help you identify some of the worries on your heart?
- When you consider your own "daily launch," consider whether you are a morning or an evening person. What would it take for you to want to "pray more than sleep" if God is calling you to set the alarm earlier for your morning launch?
- Select a prayer trigger for yourself. Write it on a card and put it where you will frequently see it. If you're in a group, share your prayer trigger with the group so you can begin praying for one another.
- What people or places has God put on your heart outside of your personal circle? Think about a trigger for a place in the world that has burdened your heart for prayer.

PART THREE: PRAY WITH AUTHORITY
Chapter 5: "The 21-Day Experiment"
- Is there a verse that "came alive" for you this week in your reading of John? Write that in the space below.

  _____

  _____

- Where are you finding ways to weave prayer into your days?
- Did you see God at work this week (this can be in the ordinary, small things)?

- Would it help to do the 21-Day Experiment with a friend? Notice how I "drafted" behind the strength of my running buddy. You may want to call each other or text your PODs.

Chapter 6: "Growing Deeper"
- What personal changes, if any, do you notice when you are consistent with a time of prayer and Bible study? Have your family members or roommates ever commented about this?
- I mentioned the *Key Word Study Bible*, my "Big Fat Greek Bible," as a tool that works well for me. Are there Bible study aids or resources that have helped you? A particular version of the Bible?
- What tips mentioned in this book have been helpful to you (e.g., the daily themes, the Chubby Book)?
- Discuss the value of concentrating on the process of prayer more than the outcome.

PART FOUR: AGREE WITH OTHERS IN PRAYER
Chapter 7: "Teammates"
- What is a dream that you long to see answered?
- Is there a special hope or dream you could share with your prayer partner? (This would be a good time to get a prayer partner if you don't already have one.)
- Why do you think Jesus said that the prayer of agreement is so powerful (Matthew 18:19)?
- He says He is there "with" us when we come together to pray. Why do you think He is present at these times? More than in individual prayer?

PART FIVE: ARM YOURSELF WITH SPIRITUAL STRENGTH
Chapter 8: "Temple Upkeep"

- Reflect on how your gifts, your life experiences, and even your current season of life will influence your life pattern.
- Have you considered attempting a "morning launch"? Or would you rather do an afternoon or evening launch?
- What kind of physical exercise seems to work best for you?
- What gets in the way of your attempts to bring structure to your daily life pattern? Do you have a friend or support group that could help you with this?

Chapter 9: "Strength in Weakness"

- Where do you see yourself in Elijah's story—fighting a battle, exhausted, waiting for the whisper, or back in the game?
- When you break, where do you run?
- What keeps you from hearing God's whispers?
- I talked about trying to fill the "God-shaped void" in my life with things other than God. What are your "hole fillers"?
- I also shared about my time of "wait training" while going through infertility. What are you waiting for—a long-cherished ream or answer to prayer?

PART SIX: ANSWER GOD'S CALL
Chapters 10, "Lift Up Your Eyes and Look," and 11, "So What? So That!"

- Is there a time when you have felt your heart break for the things that break God's? Did God speak to you in a whisper or a roar? What was your response?
- Ponder these questions: What are the gifts God has given you? Are you feeling called by God to serve Him in a certain way? Are you to pray? To give? To go?

Bonus Feature 2: Leader's Guide for Discussion Groups

A Note from Marilynn About the Discussion Group

You are feeling called to go deeper in this journey in prayer, aren't you? How do I know? First, you bought a book about learning to hear God's voice. Second, you're curious about how to inspire others to take this journey with you.

This is a good starting point in your role as leader. The rewards of traveling this journey together with a team far outweigh doing it alone. I don't know your name, how long you've had a relationship with God, your family life, your talents, your challenges, your fears, the mountains you've overcome, the dreams you hold dear, or even your failures. But I encourage you to bring all of yourself, strengths and weaknesses, into this journey. You will be a better leader if you start by being real with God and transparent with others.

My guess is you are already beginning to think of a few friends you would like to invite to hear God's voice together through prayer. The single most important step you will take in preparing for this experience is to begin praying now for those who will be in your group. I have prayed all along that this book would fall into the hands of people who need it the most. Some are longtime believers looking for a fresh breeze of the Holy Spirit. Others are beginners in their relationship with Christ. Of one thing I am certain: someone out there needs your prayer.

Ask God to help you select the members of your group. Before forming a group, I always pray, *Lord, show me who is on Your heart.* Once I prayed about inviting two women I barely knew to join our group. I happened to run into both women on the same day and each agreed to be part of the group. Expect similar "divine intersections" as you form the group.

Experience has shown me that groups function best with eight to twelve members—too many more than that, and the quality of discussion suffers. Try to gather a variety of participants, even if you are all women or all men. I've just completed this prayer journey with a small group of women who represent differing ages, stages, and even neighborhoods. The joke was that we were "some white, some black, and some blonde."

It also works best to have people who are at different places in their relationship with Christ. Sometimes spiritual seekers breathe fresh life into a group with their honest questions. The more seasoned veterans in prayer find their wisdom is valuable to the newer or younger believers.

Whether you are a group of young moms, college students, business co-workers, church members, or even those serving in the armed forces, the format will work because it's simple. It's designed for people with busy lives who want to learn how to make room for a prayer life that works.

I encourage you, as the leader, to prepare by reading the book in advance. Even if you can't read the entire book first, remember that it's vitally important for you to stay a step ahead of your group. Read the assignment and be prepared to answer any discussion questions for yourself before you share them with the group.

Each week has four basic elements:

1. Getting Started
2. Discussion
3. Homework Assignments
4. Closing Prayer

There will be some variety from week to week as to what's included in some of the elements, but the basic format will be the same. The discussion is an important part of your time together. It will do two things: bring up insights from the reading and encourage group members to open up to one another. Take some time in advance to reflect on your own answers to the questions.

I've included some general time guidelines to help you plan your sessions. The time needed for each segment will vary based on the group size and liveliness of the discussion. Don't worry if your group doesn't get to all the questions. By faithfully preparing the weekly discussions and praying for the group, you are communicating that, for eight weeks, this is worth their best energy. Seeking God wholeheartedly is a huge factor in the success of your group.

LET'S GET STARTED: LAUNCHING YOUR DISCUSSION GROUP

You will want to consider these thoughts before you begin to talk to others about a prayer discussion group:

- Do you want to use the Leader's Guide as an eight-week study or at a retreat? The guide is structured as an eight-week study, but if you want to use it at a retreat, ask everyone to read the book in advance and come prepared to discuss.

- It also works well to have a retreat as a wrap-up session after completing the seven weeks of meeting together. You might want to order my companion DVD. This can be obtained by ordering from my website, http://marilynnchadwick.com. You can also use this to accompany your discussion group.

- Who will you invite? Have you sensed God nudging you to invite someone? List them below. (Eight to twelve members is ideal.)

_____

_____

_____

_____

- Decide when you will meet, and where you will hold your meetings. Your home? A church? Your office? A dormitory?

- Consider name tags if the members don't know one another.

- Will you have refreshments? Will you take turns providing them?

- Remind members to bring their Bibles. Tell them the cost of *Sometimes He Whispers Sometimes He Roars* and that you will have their books at the first meeting.

- Along with the books, you may want to purchase copies of the Chubby Book introduced in Chapter 4. A Chubby Book is my term for any ordinary spiral-bound booklet of 3x5 index cards found in grocery or office supply stores.

◆

Week One

It's important to have the books ready to hand out at the first meeting so people can begin reading right away. Collect money for the books and encourage everyone to mark the dates for the next seven meetings. Ask for a volunteer to create a list with phone numbers and e-mail addresses.

GETTING STARTED (15–20 MINUTES)

If you have a diverse group or members who don't know one another well, you might want to begin by having them introduce themselves: their name, their family, and a favorite hobby. If they already know one another, you might have them mention their name and one fact that no one knows about them. You could use both of these introductions for a group that is diverse, making sure that they give their name each time they give a response. Go over the following ground rules with the group (feel free to add your own):

- Remind them that what is said in the group stays in the group—confidentiality is key to building trust.
- Commitment is important. Faithfulness in homework and attending the meetings is important for this experience.
- Agree to start on time and end on time. Decide as a group how long your meetings should last. An hour and a half works well for most groups.
- Remind them that any question is a good question. This is especially important if you have spiritual seekers who are new to Bible study and prayer.

Ask what they are hoping to get from this eight-week experience. This will help you guide the group better and understand each person's needs.

If you've read the book, take a few minutes to briefly share with the group why you were inspired to begin the group. Share one thing from the book that sparked your interest.

DISCUSSION (25–30 MINUTES)

The following question will serve as an icebreaker for the group to get to know one another. It also sets up the first week's reading assignment: "Describe a time you may have heard God's voice. Did this cause you to take action in any way?"

- As the leader, be prepared to answer this question first. It gives others time to think about their own answers. Plus, you will benefit from the personal reflection on how God has worked in your own life.
- Try to keep your answer to around three minutes. Time yourself—it's longer than you think.

HOMEWORK ASSIGNMENT (5–10 MINUTES)

- Read Chapters 1 and 2 for the next meeting. Answer the Personal Reflection Questions on page 189.
- Watch for signs of God at work. These signs could be answered prayer, a burden to pray for someone, or a "God moment." (Leader: Note one of your own in the space below. Be ready to share it with the group next week.)

_____

_____

- Be prepared to discuss the Personal Reflection Questions for Chapters 1 and 2.
- Remember to bring a Bible to the next group meeting.

CLOSING PRAYER (10–15 MINUTES)

- Close with prayer or ask someone in the group who is comfortable with this to close the group in a short prayer.
- Watch expectantly for God to be at work over the next seven weeks. And be sure to guard your own strength by making time for personal study, prayer, and rest.

✦

WEEK TWO

GETTING STARTED (10–15 MINUTES)

Group members were encouraged to be on the lookout for God at work since the last meeting. Allow for time to share any of these "God moments." Phrase the questions something like this:

- Where did you see God at work this week?
- Were you inspired to pray or take action as a result of this encounter?

DISCUSSION (30–35 MINUTES)

Discuss last week's reading and answers to the Personal Reflections Questions:

- How would you describe your prayer life: fueled by crisis or daily and powerful?

- What fear or worry is causing you to pray more fervently? What are a few things you've already tried besides prayer in order to solve the problem?
- How might you turn that worry into a prayer? Is there a verse from the Bible that gives you hope in this circumstance?

Focus on 1 Kings 19:9–13:

Have the group turn in their Bibles to 1 Kings 19. Set up the discussion about what led to Elijah hearing God's whisper. Remind the group of the fierce battle he had with the prophets of Baal in 1 Kings 18, and how he ran, exhausted and desperate, to the place where he had always encountered God, Mount Horeb. Have someone read 1 Kings 19:9–13 aloud.

> And the Word of the Lord came to him: "What are you doing here Elijah?" He replied, "I have been very zealous for the Lord God Almighty. The Israelites have rejected your covenant, broken down your altars, and put your prophets to death with the sword. I am the only one left, and now they are trying to kill me, too."

> The Lord said, "Go out and stand on the mountain in the presence of the Lord for the Lord is about to pass by. Then a great and powerful wind tore the mountains apart and shattered the rocks before the Lord, but the Lord was not in the wind. After the wind there was an earthquake. After the earthquake came a fire. And after the fire came a gentle whisper. When Elijah heard it, he pulled his cloak over his face and went out and stood at the mouth of the cave. Then a voice said to him, "What are you doing here, Elijah?"

Discuss 1 Kings 19:15–20:

- Where is your "Mount Horeb," a place where you feel close to God? (Leader: Write your own answer here and be ready to start the discussion.)

- When have you heard God whisper to you during a time of personal brokenness like Elijah? (Leader: Note your answer here so you might be prepared to share it.)

HOMEWORK ASSIGNMENT (5–10 MINUTES)

This week's assignment will set the tone for the rest of the prayer journey. Remind the group that since we are not carbon copies, each of us will approach God a little differently. Group members will benefit from getting alone for a time of reflection to make their lists after reading Chapters 3, "The List," and 4, "The Chubby Book Method." Some people will have long lists—others, short ones. The way we are wired by God influences how we pray.

- Read Chapters 3 and 4 for the next meeting.
- After making your prayer list, try to carve out a quiet hour during your week, using the instructions in Chapter 4.
- Purchase Chubby Books to bring to the next meeting. (Leader: Unless you have already purchased them. The group will need them for the next week's homework.)
- Be prepared to share your answers to the Personal Reflection Questions in the next meeting.

CLOSING PRAYER (10–15 MINUTES)

Close in prayer or ask a group member to pray.

✦

WEEK THREE

GETTING STARTED (10–15 MINUTES)

This week, you will ask group members to share impressions after making their lists. There is actually scientific evidence for the benefits of listing one's worries. I once read an article in the *Chicago Tribune* about a team of University of Chicago psychological scientists who found that high school and college students who jotted down their worries for ten minutes prior to an exam performed markedly better, with the average score improving by almost an entire letter grade.

Open by asking these questions:
- Did you find it helpful to write down your worries in the form of a prayer list?
- Who would be willing to share one of the prayer needs from his or her list?
- What would it look like for this prayer to be answered?

DISCUSSION (20–30 MINUTES)

In the book, I referred to fear and worry as my "twin demons." I also talked about learning "how to harness the energy of worry for the purpose of prayer."

Encourage your group to ponder Paul's words to the Philippians from the New International Version:

> Do not be anxious about anything, but in everything, by prayer and petition, with thanksgiving, present your requests to God. And the peace of God, which transcends all

understanding, will guard your hearts and minds in Christ Jesus. (Philippians 4:6–7)

Verse discussion:
- Paul gives some tools for battling worry. Talk about the different kinds of prayer mentioned in the verse: prayer, petition, thanksgiving. They may remember from their reading that the word for *petition* can mean a prayer for specific benefits. The first time the word *prayer* is mentioned in this verse, it describes a more general type of prayer.
- Ask members to spend five minutes writing down things for which they are thankful—a "thank-you list." Use the inside back cover of the Chubby Books (which they were to bring or you were to provide today) for the "thank-you list."
- After writing the "thank-you list," explore with the group why the act of thanksgiving could be a weapon against worry.

Discuss last week's reading and answers to the Personal Reflection Questions, Chapters 3, 4:
- Is your personality more of an adventurer who enjoys a little chaos or someone who is structured and orderly?
- Reflect on the value of listing specific prayer concerns. Did the exercise of making the list help you identify some of the worries on your heart?
- When you consider your own "daily launch," consider whether you are a morning or an evening person. What would it take for you to want to "pray more than sleep" if God is calling you to set the alarm earlier for your morning launch?
- Select a prayer trigger for yourself. Share your prayer trigger with the group so you can begin praying for one another.

- What people or places has God put on your heart outside of your "personal circle"? Think about a trigger for a place in the world that has burdened your heart for prayer.

Read this excerpt about praying beyond our personal circles from page 34 in Chapter 2, "Keep Watch":

As I continued to remind God that I was available to pray for His world, I became increasingly alert to what was happening in the world beyond my own walls. I might read about a terrorist attack in India or the persecution of believers in China. An Internet article about human suffering would catch my eye. I would pray briefly about the need. Often I would become alert to further mention of the need, and thus be reminded to pray—quietly, simply, again and again.

Day-to-day living took on new vibrancy as watchful prayer made me more attuned to the human suffering along my path. I would strike up a conversation with a young mother in the grocery store, only to find she was a victim of domestic violence. In the Phoenix airport I sat next to a young soldier named Jesse. He was headed for Alaska and then on to Afghanistan. I promised him I'd pray, and now "Soldier Jesse" has a spot on my prayer list. Were there more people in pain or was I just seeing the world through new eyes?

Help the group begin to explore their own heart for the world with the following questions:
- Are you willing to pray for God to burden your heart for needs beyond your own walls? You can begin by being alert to pray for

people you bump into in your daily life—a child's teacher, a co-worker having family problems. Note those people here.

_____

_____

- Is there a nation or place that God has put on your heart? What caused you to be interested? (Family originated there, friends from that country, travel, news article?)
- What did you think of the "Sudan Sam" story? China's Reverend Sam Lamb? Is there a way you could put a similar "face on a nation"?
- Maybe the group would agree together to add one particular nation to their lists as a group prayer project. Agree to pray for this nation on a given day of the week.

HOMEWORK ASSIGNMENT (10–15 MINUTES)

Some group members are familiar with doing a daily Bible reading, but for others this will be their first experience with a regular Bible and prayer time. Allow time to explain homework and answer questions. Be familiar enough with Chapter 5 to talk them through the 21-Day Experiment. Have the group pick a start and a stop date if they want to do the exercise together.

Demonstrate how to use a Chubby Book (see the "Quick-Start Method for Using the Chubby Book" later in the appendices).

- Read Chapter 5.
- Go over instructions on pages 76–77 in Chapter 5 about the 21-Day Experiment in prayer. (Leader: If any group members are new to reading the Bible, they may benefit from the "PRA" format: P, pray before reading for God to open the mind to His

Word; R, reflect while reading ["What is the text saying? What is it saying to me?"]; A, what kind of action am I to take as the result of my reading?)

- Be prepared to discuss the Personal Reflection Questions for Chapter 5.

CLOSING PRAYER (10–15 MINUTES)

Encourage each group member to pray aloud, going around the circle. Ask them to pray a one-sentence prayer about a couple of items on their list—maybe one need from their personal circle and one for the larger world. Then pause a few seconds before the next person prays. As leader, end with a brief prayer to complete the time together.

✦

WEEK FOUR

GETTING STARTED (10–15 MINUTES)

One of the reasons for doing the 21-Day Experiment is to build a habit of spending time in God's Word and prayer on a daily basis. This helps us get to know God better, builds our trust in Him. This, in turn, energizes our prayers. Romans 10:17 reminds us that faith "comes from hearing the Word." That's why it's so worth the effort to read God's Word on a daily basis.

DISCUSSION (30–35 MINUTES)
Focus on Matthew 8:5–10, 13:

When Jesus had entered Capernaum, a centurion came to him, asking for help. "Lord," he said, "my servant lies at home paralyzed and in terrible suffering." Jesus said to him, "I will go and heal him." The centurion replied, "Lord, I do not deserve to have you come under my roof. But just say the word and my servant will be healed. For I myself am a man under authority, with soldiers under me. I tell this one, 'Go,' and he goes; and that one, 'Come,' and he comes. I say to my servant, 'Do this,' and he does it." When Jesus heard this, he was astonished and said to those following him, "I tell you the truth, I have not found anyone in Israel with such great faith. . . . Then Jesus said to the centurion, "Go! It will be done just as you believed it would." And his servant was healed at that very hour.

Answer these questions:
- What does it mean to take Jesus at His Word?
- What is the relationship between authority and faith?
- How is reading His Word related to hearing His voice?

Discuss Personal Reflection Questions, Chapter 5:
Spend some time talking with your group about their 21-Day Experiment. Are they beginning to experience a running conversation with God? Did anything from Chapter 5 especially speak to them? Be alert to where members are in their own spiritual journey. This might be the first serious Bible reading effort for some in your group.

- Is there a verse that "came alive" for you this week in your reading of John?
- Where are you finding ways to weave prayer into your days?
- Did you see God at work this week (perhaps in the ordinary, small things)?

- Would it help to do the 21-Day Experiment with a friend? Remember how I "drafted" behind the strength of my running buddy. You may want to call each other or text your PODs (prayers on demand).

HOMEWORK ASSIGNMENT (5–10 MINUTES)
- Continue the 21-Day Experiment: memorize one verse from your reading in John.
- Watch for God at work around you. Are you being prompted to pray for people or places? You may want to add them to your list if you feel like ongoing prayer is needed.
- Read Chapter 6, "Growing Deeper."
- Be ready to discuss the Personal Reflection Questions for Chapter 6.

CLOSING PRAYER (10–15 MINUTES)
Go around the circle and ask each person to pray a short prayer (a sentence or two) for the person on his or her left. Encourage the group to pray that they will see the world around them with "new eyes." Ask for a volunteer who would be willing to close with final prayer.

✦

WEEK FIVE

GETTING STARTED (15–20 MINUTES)
My running buddy and I try to stick with our morning routine, even when the weather is cold. We find that on days when the temperature dips into the low teens, the cold becomes bearable after

about five minutes of running. By the end of our half hour, we may be sweating. Why? Our motor (the heart) has warmed up our body.

I've noticed the same thing happens when reading God's Word. I may wake up to the cold weather of despair, worry, guilt, or fatigue. But something happens when I spend time in the Word, reading, reflecting, searching for spiritual food. Within minutes, my heart has lifted. It's as though I've warmed my heart with God's Word. The faith engine is running, and I find myself believing that God can and will work in the things that concern me.

Building your trust in God is like any relationship. It happens over time and is reinforced by seeing Him at work in your life. In John 6:29, Jesus tells us that the "work of God is this: to believe in the one he has sent." My mission when I wake up each day is to fire up my engine—my physical body, so I can do the things I am called to do that day. Likewise, I fire up my faith engine, so I can pray with confidence, trusting Jesus and the truth of God's Word for the needs I see all around me. The point of it all is not just prayer. It is faith.

Favorite verses:
These are some of my favorite verses about faith. I have memorized them. Ask four people to read a verse. What strikes the group about these verses? How can faith be both a gift and a fight?

- "For it is by grace you have been saved, through faith—and this not from yourselves, it is the gift of God—not by works, so that no one can boast" (Ephesians 2:8–9).
- "Now faith is being sure of what we hope for and certain of what we do not see" (Hebrews 11:1).

- "And without faith it is impossible to please God, because anyone who comes to him must believe he exists and that he rewards those who earnestly seek him" (Hebrews 11:6).
- "Fight the good fight of the faith" (1 Timothy 6:12a).

DISCUSSION (25–30 MINUTES)

Read this excerpt from pages 77–78:

> As I continued to practice my daily habit of reading God's Word and prayer, I noticed . . . that I worried less—especially since it was becoming a reflex to channel my worries into prayers. By bringing my fears, weaknesses, sins, problems, worries, dreams, hopes, and heart's desires straight to my encounters with God, I gave Him first shot at filling those needs. . . . I also seemed to have fewer bursts of temper. After all, when I didn't see it as my job to play God and try to fix everybody, I was less likely to get angry when they didn't change according to my plans. And with all the energy I didn't spend on worry and anger, I seemed to have more energy for the work God *had* called me to do, whether at home with my family, leading Bible studies, or being available for His work in the world.

Discuss Personal Reflection Questions, Chapter 6:
- What personal changes, if any, do you notice when you are consistent with a time of prayer and Bible study? Have your family members or roommates ever commented about this?
- I mentioned the *Key Word Study Bible*, my "Big Fat Greek Bible," as a tool that works well for me. Are there Bible study

aids or resources that have helped you? A particular version of the Bible?

- What tips mentioned in this book have been helpful to you (e.g., the daily themes, Chubby Book)?
- Discuss the value of concentrating on the process of prayer more than the outcome.

Discuss some ways The Lord's Prayer can be applied to one's prayer life: Encourage the group to comment on the Chapter 6 teaching on The Lord's Prayer as a recipe for a well-balanced prayer "diet." What other ways have they found that it shapes their prayers? You might ask these questions:

- Have you been nudged to pray The Lord's Prayer for a person or place?
- Is there a prayer need that has required persistence on your part?
- Did anything strike you as a new or an inspiring insight about The Lord's Prayer?

Comment on the often-overlooked aspect of confession (to other believers as well as to God):
How do the verses below speak to the importance of a prayer partner? A group? Tell them that next week's reading will talk about both.

- "Therefore confess your sins to each other and pray for each other so that you may be healed" (James 5:16).
- "Encourage one another daily, as long as it is called 'Today,' so that none of you may be hardened by sin's deceitfulness" (Hebrews 3:13).

HOMEWORK ASSIGNMENT (10–15 MINUTES)

- Read Chapters 7, "Teammates," and 8, "Temple Upkeep."
- Continue the 21-Day Experiment. Be ready to discuss insights from their experience at the next meeting.
- (Leader: Assign prayer partners just for the week.) Perhaps you might text your prayer partner a verse. Or stand in agreement on a promise. Or confess a shortcoming. Try this out for a week.
- Spend some quiet time reflecting on priorities—take a first stab at putting a life pattern on paper. Refer to pages 132–133 in Chapter 8 for guidelines.
- Be prepared to discuss the Personal Reflection Questions from Chapters 7 and 8.

CLOSING PRAYER (10–15 MINUTES)

Think of a creative way to incorporate the following elements of The Lord's Prayer into the closing prayer. You could pray for a need in your community or world using the format. Maybe a different person could cover each aspect of the prayer:

- Thanks, praise
- God's kingdom on earth
- Daily needs
- Confession and forgiveness
- Guidance and protection
- Deliverance or rescue

Consider having the group set their cell phone alarms to pray The Lord's Prayer "A Minute a Day at Noon" for a nation.

✦

WEEK SIX

GETTING STARTED (5–10 MINUTES)

God speaks through His Word and His works. We hear God's voice when we read His Word. But He has also left His finger-prints on every particle of His creation. Since the creation of the world, Paul tells us in Romans 1:20, "God's invisible quali-ties—his eternal power and divine nature—have been clearly seen, being understood from what has been made, so that men are without excuse."

My friend Allyson says she experiences God most powerfully in settings where she "feels small," for instance, in the mountains. Janet is inspired to trust God when she looks at the nighttime sky: "If God can make the solar system, then surely He can handle my problems." My husband, David, loves to add worship music to his Bible study times—drawing strength from God's Word put to song. In short, God speaks your language. He knows how you are made—you are His design.

DISCUSSION (40–50 MINUTES)

Encourage your group to answer these questions:

- When do you sense you can most easily hear God's voice? (In worship, when hearing personal stories, while serving the poor, etc.)
- How does God's Word come alive for you? (In a large-group set-ting, reading quietly, small-group discussion.)

Talk about the value of having a prayer partner:
Early Christians were sometimes called "The People of the Way." One of the benefits of community is that we can encourage one another as we build new habits. Let's consider how we can challenge one another to develop a world-changing faith in Christ.

Ask the group to look at Matthew 18:19–20. Jesus says in Matthew 18 that there is great power in the prayer of agreement. "I tell you that if two of you on earth agree about anything you ask for, it will be done for you by my Father in heaven. For where two or three come together in my name, there am I with them."

Discuss their answers to last week's Personal Reflection Questions (in two parts):

Chapter 7, "Teammates":
- What is a dream that you long to see answered?
- Is there a special hope or dream you could share with your prayer partner? (This would be a good time to get a prayer partner if you don't already have one.)
- Why do you think Jesus said that the prayer of agreement is so powerful (Matthew 18:19)?
- He says He is there "with" us when we come together to pray. Why do you think He is present at these times? More than in individual prayer?

Discuss life patterns:
Your group members are beginning to develop life patterns that make room for prayer and hearing God's voice. My prayer partner, Beth, says she likes to get her "marching orders" first thing in

the morning. My husband, David, feels the same way. No matter how much work he faces, he begins his morning with time in God's Word and prayer. Others, like mothers of small children, find their "launch" is most effective when children go down for their first nap.

Chapter 8, "Temple Upkeep":
- Reflect on how your gifts, your life experiences, and even your current season of life will influence your life pattern.
- Have you considered attempting a "morning launch"? Or would you rather do an afternoon or evening launch?
- What kind of physical exercise seems to work best for you?
- What gets in the way of your attempts to bring structure to your daily life pattern? Do you have a friend or support group that could help you with this?

Discuss their "power hours":
Everyone's answers will be a little different, but it helps to think about what kind of daily pattern is best suited to help each person stay connected to God's voice. A life pattern should reflect one's personality, season of life, experiences, gifts, and talents.

- Have the group share their ideas about what's important for a healthy life pattern: include a balance of time in God's Word and prayer, service to others, rest, family time, friend time, solitude, and personal refreshment.
- What are their most effective hours of the day—their "power hours"?
- Talk briefly about their work/rest ratio. Do they need to give

more attention to their "temple upkeep" routine to keep the machinery working well?

HOMEWORK ASSIGNMENT (5 MINUTES)
- Complete the 21-Day Experiment. Try to take some time to be quiet this week. Think about what you have learned about hearing God's voice during the 21-Day Experiment.
- Read Chapter 9, "Strength in Weakness."
- Be prepared to discuss Personal Reflection Questions for Chapter 9.

CLOSING PRAYER (10–15 MINUTES)
If you had the group break into prayer partners last week, you might want to encourage the prayer partners to pray for each other during the closing prayer.

✦

WEEK SEVEN

GETTING STARTED (5–10 MINUTES)
"If God is God, He can speak to any heart at any time. For Jesus to talk to you, you don't have to be virtuous. You just have to be quiet." (Mr. Black to Mr. White in Cormac McCarthy's *The Sunset Limited*, a two-man play [2006] and a movie [2011].)

Your group members were encouraged to make some time for quiet reflection after completing their 21-Day Experiment. It helps to remember that when building a habit of daily Bible reading and prayer, it's more about a relationship with God than ritual.

Jesus talked to His disciples about the importance of this

relationship in John 15. "If a man remains in me and I in him, he will bear much fruit; apart from me you can do nothing" (John 15:5). He added, "If you remain in me and my words remain in you, ask whatever you wish, and it will be given to you" (verse 7). The point is this: if you spend much time with the Lord, studying His Word, you're more likely to be praying according to His will.

DISCUSSION (25–30 MINUTES)

Encourage your group to answer the following question upon completion of the 21-Day Experiment; but before they do, encourage each person to reflect on his or her answer in advance, and limit the response to three minutes. This is a good skill and will sharpen their summary.

- Did you hear God's voice in the pages of the book of John? How did you respond to what you heard? (You told someone else, gave something away, served someone, released a fear, repented of sin, etc.)

Discuss their answers to last week's Personal Reflection Questions:
In reading Chapter 9, "Strength in Weakness," where did you see yourself in Elijah's story—in the battle, exhausted, waiting for God's voice, or back in the game?

- Is there something in your life that keeps you from hearing God's whispers? Think about the things you might run to instead of God (shopping, food, sleep, friends, isolation, sin, or addictions).
- I talk about trying to fill the "God-shaped void" in my life with things other than God. What are your "hole fillers"?

- I shared about my time of "wait training" while going through infertility. What are you waiting for—a long-cherished dream or answered prayer?

HOMEWORK ASSIGNMENT (15–20 MINUTES)
Read Chapters 10, "Lift Up Your Eyes and Look," and 11, "So What? So That!" Most of us feel compelled to take some kind of action after opening our eyes to the needs around us. Consider ways you could serve together. Be prepared to discuss these at the last meeting. Here are some possibilities:

- Pray a minute a day for a need or a nation. Research that nation and learn more about how to specifically pray. *Operation World*[1] is among the many great resources to help you understand strategic prayer for the needs of the world.
- Explore mission websites that explain ways to donate or volunteer. Become part of a local church and find out where they are serving.
- Visit a homeless shelter. Consider tutoring the children or leading a *Sometimes He Whispers Sometimes He Roars* discussion group for the mothers. Your group can put what they've learned into practice.
- Explore a local or an international project you could financially support together—a student sponsorship, a grinding mill, or other income-producing projects for a village (see "My Favorite Resources," page 231).
- (Leader: For the last session, consider a longer meeting with a meal at the end. My group found it worked well for everyone to bring a brunch dish to share.)
- As you complete the final chapters in the book, reflect on the

practical as well as spiritual value of the group's experience together.

- Be prepared to discuss answers to Personal Reflection Questions for Chapters 10 and 11.

CLOSING PRAYER (10–15 MINUTES)

Ask the group to pray for God to speak to them in the next week about turning their eyes outward. Pray for His guidance in any next steps.

✦

WEEK EIGHT

GETTING STARTED (10–15 MINUTES)

Most people want to believe that their life on earth makes a difference. Even children long to know their purpose. My husband's father, the late Dr. Howard Chadwick, a minister for seventy years, used to encourage our three children to search for their life's calling. "Look around you at the needs you see in the world," he would tell them. "Then take an honest look at your own gifts and talents. Your calling may be found where the two intersect." Though he is no longer with us, we still refer to "Granddaddy Chadwick's rule" for discovering your life's mission.

The group has been talking for several weeks about developing their hearts to hear God's voice. But if that relationship takes us no further than our own needs, then so what? God saves us, sets us free, and loves us—so that we can be His hands and feet in a broken and dying world. We yearn to know that we are good for something.

Ephesians 2:10 tells us we are His workmanship, or "masterpiece," created or "born anew" in "Christ Jesus to do good works, which God prepared in advance for us to do." It's only logical that He would hardwire into each of us the necessary set of gifts and skills to fulfill our calling.

DISCUSSION (40–50 MINUTES)
Train yourself to sustain yourself:
It's especially important to keep listening to God's voice and stay connected to Him on a daily basis—especially when we move out of our comfort zone to serve others. More than ever, we need His guidance, wisdom, and protection as we walk among the broken and hurting—especially those without Christ. The Bible reminds us that it's not by our might or power that we do the works of God, but "by His Spirit" (Zechariah 4:6). We are not designed to do this alone.

Ask your group to briefly discuss ways they will commit to staying strong for the long haul.

- Daily study of the Bible and prayer
- Continuing to develop their life pattern
- Tithing their income and always looking for creative ways to give to God's work
- Praying with a prayer partner; meeting with a prayer group
- Being part of a church that preaches the Gospel and has a heart for missions; finding ways to serve the "least and lost"
- Remaining alert to God's voice throughout the day; praying for open doors to share the good news
- Other

Discuss answers to Personal Reflection Questions:
Talk with your group about listening for God's calling on their lives. For the last several weeks, they've been training their hearts to hear His voice. What are they hearing from God about their calling?

Chapter 10, "Lift Up Your Eyes and Look":

• Is there a time when you have felt your heart break for the things that break God's?
• Did God speak to you in a whisper or a roar?
• What was your response?

Chapter 11, "So What? So That!":

Read 1 Peter 4:10 and comment on the importance of spiritual gifts. "Each one should use whatever gift he has received from God to serve others, faithfully administering God's grace in its various forms."

• What are the gifts God has given you? Think about spiritual gifts, life experiences, skills, talents, etc. (You may want to read Romans 12:4–8 for a list of spiritual gifts.)
• Are you feeling called by God to use these gifts to serve Him in a certain way? Are you to pray? To give? To go?

Final reflections—So What? or So That!:
Your group was encouraged to think of ways they could serve together. Some possible ideas were mentioned in week seven. Discuss their thoughts about the following ideas so they might choose one for the future.

- Pray a minute a day for a nation. Research that nation. Your group was encouraged to read *Operation World*, a great resource to equip oneself for strategic prayer for every nation in the world.
- Explore mission websites that explain ways to donate or volunteer.
- Visit a homeless shelter. Consider tutoring the children or leading a *Sometimes He Whispers Sometimes He Roars* discussion group for the mothers. Your group can put what they've learned into practice.
- Explore a local or an international project you could financially support together—a student sponsorship, a grinding mill, or other income-producing projects for a village. (See Bonus Feature 5, "My Favorite Resources.")

Are there other ideas they'd like to consider?

Expectations:

In the first session, you asked the participants what they were hoping to get from this eight-week experience. Have they experienced any personal changes? How has their view of the world changed? Were their expectations for this study fulfilled? If not, what are they still looking for? This might be a new avenue for the discussion group.

CLOSING PRAYER (15–20 MINUTES)

It was a common practice in the New Testament to lay hands on fellow believers and pray for them as they moved out in service.

Spend some time in a prayer of commissioning for your group as they commit to serve God. The group might gather around each member—one at a time—and lay hands on this person, praying for his or her calling. Or go around in a circle and have each member put a hand on the shoulder of the person on the right, asking for the Holy Spirit to empower his or her commitment to service.

As leader, you may want to close in a prayer, commissioning the group as a whole.

Either begin or end with the brunch, lunch, or refreshments.

Bonus Feature 3: Quick-Start Method for Using the Chubby Book

The Chubby Book method is a great way to make your prayer list part of your daily life. You can use it along with any Bible reading plan. It works especially well with the 21-Day Experiment in Chapter 5, since it keeps your 3x5 cards together in one wire-bound booklet. I find that by putting my daily list and a verse or two from God's Word in the Chubby Book, I can take my prayers "out of the closet" and into the world. This method is well suited for real life on the go. It's simple, it's sustainable, and it leaves plenty of room for God to work. You can tailor the Chubby Book method to suit your personality. Here's what works for me:

1. I open the Chubby Book flat so I have two 3x5 cards—one on the top and one on the bottom. I refer to my Master List from Chapter 4 (I like to keep my list on the back page of my Prayer Journal).

2. I write the needs from that day of the week on the bottom card. I also make a column next to my list and label it "POD." These are my "prayers on demand," prayers not on my list that are on my heart. I also put the theme for the day at the top of my list.

3. I spend time reading God's Word with whatever Bible reading plan I am using. If you start with the 21-Day Experiment, you will be in the book of John.

4. After a prayerful reading, I copy a verse or two that seemed to "light up" for me. I write these verses on the top card so I can glance at the verses and my prayer list at the same time.

5. I quietly reflect on the verses. I often pray those verses for each need on my list. I pray for God to meet my own needs through His promises in these verses. Sometimes I will go over my list and meditate on my verses while I fold clothes or do dishes. This reminds me to use moments in my day for prayer.

6. I take the Chubby Book with me throughout my day so I can glance at the list and keep the Bible verses and prayer needs foremost in my mind. This works well if I have a long drive across town. I can pray for my list while waiting for an appointment or even during a workout. I keep a running conversation with God.

7. My absolute favorite is to grab an afternoon walk in a pretty location and go over my list or memorize the verses while walking. You may find, as I do, that sometimes you will sing the verses (where no one can hear!)—that's probably how David wrote the book of Psalms.

The Chubby Book

John 20:31

"But these are written that
you may believe that Jesus
is the Christ, the son of God,
and that by believing you
may have life in His name."

Daily Theme: PRAISE

	POD's
Jessie	Kris and Marisa
SEEDs Scholars	Mom's healing
Dominique	JB's calling
Mideast: Egypt	Michael's meet
Soldier Jesse: Afghanistan	peace: Sudan
Jonathan & family	ALARM: Emily
Women battling infertility	

Bonus Feature 4: My "A-List": Prayer Lifelines

God used the verses below to lead me in my journey. I hope they will become signposts along the way for you in yours.

1. *Alert:* "Don't worry about anything; instead, pray about everything. Tell God what you need and thank Him for all He has done. If you do this, you will experience God's peace, which is far more wonderful than the human mind can understand. His peace will guard your hearts and minds as you live in Christ Jesus" (Philippians 4:6–7, NLT).

2. *Ask:* "In the morning, O LORD, you hear my voice; in the morning I lay my requests before you and wait in expectation" (Psalm 5:3).

3. *Attentive:* "My sheep listen to my voice; I know them, and they follow me" (John 10:27).

4. *Alone:* "When you pray, go into your room, close the door and pray to your Father, who is unseen. Then your Father, who sees what is done in secret, will reward you" (Matthew 6:6).

5. *Agree:* "If two of you on earth agree about anything you ask for, it will be done for you by my Father in heaven" (Matthew 18:19).

6. *Admit:* "Confess your sins to each other and pray for each other so that you may be healed" (James 5:16).

7. *Armor:* "Put on the full armor of God so that you can take your stand against the devil's schemes . . . And pray in the Spirit on all occasions with all kinds of prayers and requests" (Ephesians 6:11, 18).

8. *Abide:* "If you abide in Me, and My words abide in you, ask whatever you wish, and it will be done for you" (John 15:7, NASB).

9. *Action:* "If you spend yourselves in behalf of the hungry and satisfy the needs of the oppressed, then your light will rise in the darkness, and your night will become like the noonday" (Isaiah 58:10).

10. *Abound:* "And God is able to make all grace abound to you, so that in all things at all times, having all that you need, you will abound in every good work" (2 Corinthians 9:8).

Bonus Feature 5: My Favorite Resources

Over the last thirty years I've lost count of the number of books I've read on prayer. These remain constant—never far from my nightstand.

- *Hebrew-Greek Key Word Study Bible* (NIV or NASB) by Spiros Zodhiates. If I could own only one Bible, this would be it.
- *How to Pray* by R. A. Torrey. Written in 1900, this short but powerful book is my personal favorite on the topic of prayer.
- *The Power of Prayer in a Believer's Life* by Charles H. Spurgeon. Biblical prayer guidelines from Britain's well-known nineteenth-century preacher.
- *Adventures in Prayer* by Catherine Marshall. Written nearly forty years ago, this little book gives a practical and powerful approach to prayer. Includes intriguing stories about answered prayer.
- *Why Pray?* by John DeVries. DeVries outlines in detail how prayer paved the way for the work of Mission India. Has application for your home and neighborhood.
- *Streams in the Desert* by L. B. Cowman. A classic—maybe the

most popular devotional of all time. A powerful companion to prayer and Bible study.

- YouVersion.com/download created by LifeChurch.tv. A free Bible application for your mobile device, available in fifty-five translations and more than twenty languages. Allows you to associate web media (such as videos, photos, links, and text) to any verse or passage.

ENLARGING YOUR VIEW

These books will open your eyes to the needs of the world.

- *Operation World,* 21ˢᵗ Century Edition, by Patrick Johnstone and Jason Mandryk. A valuable tool for specific prayer, country by country. (Jason Mandryk has completed a revised 7th edition *Operation World: The Definitive Prayer Guide to Every Nation.*)
- *Hope Lives: A Journey of Restoration* by Amber Van Schooneveld. A five-week Bible study on prayer and responding to God's call to serve the poor.
- *Forgiving as We've Been Forgiven: Community Practices for Making Peace* by L. Gregory Jones and Célestin Musekura. Reflections on the issue of biblical forgiveness along with the personal story of Rwandan genocide survivor and ALARM founder Célestin Musekura.
- *Left to Tell: Discovering God Amidst the Rwandan Holocaust* by Immaculée Ilibagiza. A tragic but triumphant story of how Immaculée and seven women were hidden by a Christian pastor in a tiny bathroom for ninety days while the Rwandan genocide raged.

TURN YOUR PRAYER INTO ACTION

I've seen the work of these organizations firsthand. Go on their websites for more information about how to pray, give, or go.

- ALARM (African Leadership and Reconciliation Ministries): works to develop local church leaders who then transform their communities in eight Central African countries. www.alarm-inc.org
- Samaritan's Purse: the Church Rebuilding Project in Southern Sudan has completed 422 of the 800 churches destroyed during the years of genocide. www.samaritanspurse.org
- SIM (Serving in Mission): their Basic Education Learning Centers (BELC) are educating the Southern Sudanese by training village leaders who then teach the children. www.sim.org
- United World Mission: in addition to extensive global missions, UWM offers two-year missions assignments in various parts of the world, from Europe to Africa. www.uwm.org
- Mission India: equips local Indian believers to plant churches. Children touched by their Children's Bible Club project are leading their families and entire villages to Christ. www.missionindia.org
- Christian Solidarity International: involved in compelling human rights issues worldwide, with a heart for persecuted Christians. www.csi-int.org
- Seeds of Hope: empowers dreamers to reach their educational goals so that they will transform their communities. The Seeds Scholars program provides scholarships and identifies projects that foster education and spread the Gospel. www.SeedsScholars.org

Two local Seeds of Hope projects with global impact:

- Seeds Beads: proceeds go to help women and children in northern Uganda who fled their villages after attacks by rebel groups. Women are left widowed and traumatized—children are abducted as child soldiers. The Seeds Beads project addresses the spiritual, emotional, and practical needs of these women. It provides Bible training and a supportive community, teaching women how to turn recycled paper into beautiful jewelry— made highly popular by today's fashion industry. Income from one twenty-dollar necklace will feed a widow and five children for a month! It also enables children to attend school. Seeds of Hope partners with ALARM to sell these beads. You can host a bead party or sell them at an event (www.SeedsScholars.org).

- Institute of Women's Excellence in Rwanda (IWE): the IWE school was founded by ALARM in Rwanda to address a community whose young women were in crisis. Due to the 1994 Rwandan genocide and the scourge of HIV/AIDS, many were orphaned and living on the street, often as prostitutes. This thriving secondary school provides a refuge where young women develop spiritually, emotionally, and academically. Seeds of Hope has partnered with ALARM by providing student sponsorships. Visit the Seeds website to learn more about sponsoring a student. Monthly sponsorships start at twenty-five dollars.

Acknowledgments

Every dream needs a team. Without many mentors and encouragers, this book would have been just another idea. I'm grateful for the teammates who cheered me on along the way.

My friend Janet Thoma believed in this book even before I did. She was patient to let the idea take root. When the time was right, she helped me capture this decade-long prayer journey in book form. Janet, I pray your legacy bears lasting fruit.

Beth Frye has been prayer partner extraordinaire—we forged strong prayer habits and friendship as we sent "PODs" daily for our families and for the world. And without my faithful friend and running buddy, Susan Flynn, I'd never have been awake and alert in the morning for prayer in the first place.

Trusted friends provided valuable feedback and lots of prayer along the way. Judy Forrest spent hours reviewing the manuscript. Her enthusiasm for the project inspired the creation of a Leader's Guide. Lisa Allen and the "Thursday Girls" were a great prayer laboratory. Jan Austin, as always, gave wise counsel.

Philis Boultinghouse, Amanda Demastus, and the great staff

at Simon & Schuster (Howard Books) believed in this first-time author, something of a miracle in itself. Thanks, Philis, for patiently guiding me through the ropes and for challenging me to write with my reader in mind. To Nicci Jordan Hubert for bringing elements of structure to my work. And of course to Jonathan Merkh, who opened the door in the first place.

I remain inspired by the Forest Hill Church family. Thirty years ago, who could have imagined what God would accomplish through that small but faithful group and their young pastor and his new bride? God has since used this passionate community of believers to reach multitudes of the least and lost in Charlotte and to "the ends of the earth."

To my mom and dad, I owe my deepest gratitude. Your unconditional and often sacrificial love always encouraged me to dream big. A model of faithfulness through fifty-plus years of marriage, you've provided a rich legacy—one I've tried to pass on to my own family. I'm also deeply thankful for my sisters, Susan and Janice. I love you dearly. And for Howard and Ramona, Carolyn and Dan. So glad I'm part of the Chadwick tribe. Dad and Mom Chadwick ever remain a source of inspiration as part of the "great cloud of witnesses." I began writing this book the very day Dad went to be with the Lord. I've sensed his presence on occasion while writing, encouraging me to press on to the finish.

I'm more thankful than words can say for my own family. Our three children, Bethany, David, and Michael, are truly gifts from God. Being your mom has been my highest calling and my great reward. Ryan, our son-in-law, has been a wonderful addition, along with grandbaby Anna Grace. Jessie, you are fast becoming like another daughter to me, too. I love each of you more than life itself.

David, you are truly my hero and the man of my dreams. I love your gentleness, your courage, and the way you treat all people the same—great or small in the world's eyes. I'll never forget what my friend said about you before our blind date. "You're going to *really* like this guy," she insisted. "To be so amazing, he is incredibly humble." I was hooked. Three decades of ministry and three children later, I'm so glad I said yes. You are everything on my "wish list" and more.

Finally, at its essence, this is a story about the faithfulness of God—all glory and honor go to my Lord and Savior Jesus Christ.

Notes

INTRODUCTION

1. Laurence Gonzales, "Deep Survival," *National Geographic Adventure*, February 2009, p. 26.

CHAPTER 2: KEEP WATCH

1. Robert Murray M'Cheyne's daily Bible reading plan was compiled more than a hundred years ago by the Scottish pastor. You may obtain a free copy through this website: http://www.pesdirect.com/calendar.pdf.

CHAPTER 3: THE LIST

1. Charles H. Spurgeon, *The Power of Prayer in a Believer's Life*, compiled and edited by Robert Hall (Lynnwood, Wash.: Emerald Books, Lance C. Wubbels, 1993), p. 168.

2. John DeVries, *Why Pray?* (Colorado Springs: Honor Books, 2005), p. 253.

3. Ryan Dunch, "Worshiping Under the Communist Eye," *Christian History and Biography*, Spring 2008, p. 22.

4. Roy E. Conwell, *Samwiil of Sudan* (Brisbane, Australia: Bethel Ministries, 1985).

Chapter 5: The 21-Day Experiment
1. R. A. Torrey, *How to Pray* (Chicago: Moody Classics), p. 8.
2. Emily Gardiner Neal, *The Healing Power of Christ* (London: Hodder and Stoughton, Ltd, 1972).
3. LifeChurch.tv, based in Edmond, Oklahoma, puts out a Bible application you can download for free. It's available in fifty-five translations and more than twenty languages. From your mobile device, go to youversion.com/download.

Chapter 6: Growing Deeper
1. David Chadwick, *The Twelve Leadership Principles of Dean Smith* (New York: Total/Sports Illustrated, 1999), p. 91.
2. Spiros Zodhiates, ed., *Hebrew-Greek Key Word Study Bible*, New International Version (Chattanooga: AMG Publishers, 1996).
3. Kenneth W. Osbeck, *Amazing Grace: 366 Inspiring Hymn Stories for Daily Devotions* (Grand Rapids: Kregel Publications, 1990), p. 17.
4. See Samaritan's Purse video about Zaki Samwiil at http://www.vimeo.com/1665714; for more information about Samaritan's Purse work in the Sudan: http://www.samaritanspurse.org/sudan.

Chapter 7: Teammates
1. R. A. Torrey, *How to Pray* (Chicago: Moody Classics), p. 22.
2. Debra Williams, D.D., "Scientific Research of Prayer: Can the Power of Prayer Be Proven?" 1999 PLIM Retreat, (c) 1999 PLIM REPORT, Vol. 8 #4 Theme: Inner Journey, Part 5 (http://www.plim.org/PrayerDeb.htm).

Chapter 8: Temple Upkeep

1. Wil Derkse, *The Rule of Benedict for Beginners: Spirituality for Daily Life,* translated from Dutch by Martin Kessler (Collegeville, Minn.: Liturgical Press, 2003).

Chapter 9: Strength in Weakness

1. C. S. Lewis, *Mere Christianity* (New York: HarperCollins, 1952).

Chapter 10: Lift Up Your Eyes and Look

1. Elie Wiesel, *Night* (New York: Bantam, 1982), p. 32.
2. C. S. Lewis, *The Lion, the Witch and the Wardrobe* (New York: Collier Books, 1978), p. 75.

Chapter 11: So What? So That!

1. Visit the Seeds of Hope website at www.SeedsScholars.org to learn more about the Seeds Scholars program and how Forest Hill launched this 501c3 organization. Seeds of Hope enables the church to intersect with our community through local and global projects. E-mail address: info@seedsscholars.org.

Afterword

1. David Chadwick, *My Father, My Friend* (Charlotte: Forest Hill Resources, 2009).
2. Kenneth W. Osbeck, *Amazing Grace: 366 Inspiring Hymn Stories for Daily Devotions* (Grand Rapids: Kregel Publications, 1990), p. 17.

Leader's Guide

1. Jason Mandryk, *Operation World* (Colorado Springs: Biblica, 2010).

Invite Marilynn Chadwick to your group study or retreat.

Order a DVD with a four-part series of Marilynn teaching her six steps to hearing the voice of God. Each thirty-minute segment will accompany the lessons in the Leader's Guide.

Order the DVD through Marilynn's website http://marilynnchadwick.com or by calling 803-548-2617.

Cost $10.00 plus shipping and handling.